International
Best Practice

A Practical Guide to Project Planning
A Step-by-step Approach

London: TSO

Published by TSO (The Stationery Office), part of Williams Lea, and
available from:

Online
www.internationalbestpractice.com
www.tsoshop.co.uk

Mail, Telephone, Fax & E-mail
TSO
PO Box 29, Norwich, NR3 1GN
Telephone orders/General enquiries: 0333 202 5070
Fax orders: 0333 202 5080
E-mail: customer.services@tso.co.uk
Textphone 0333 202 5077

TSO@Blackwell and other Accredited Agents

International Best Practice (IBP) is a framework-neutral, independent imprint of TSO. We source, create
and publish guidance which improves business processes and efficiency. We deliver an ever-expanding
range of best-practice guidance and frameworks to a global audience.

The information contained in this publication is believed to be correct at the time of manufacture. Whilst
care has been taken to ensure that the information is accurate, the publisher can accept no responsibility
for any errors or omissions or for changes to the details given.

MoP® is a registered trade mark of AXELOS Limited
MSP® is a registered trade mark of AXELOS Limited
P3M3® is a registered trade mark of AXELOS Limited
P3O® is a registered trade mark of AXELOS Limited
PRINCE2® is a registered trade mark of AXELOS Limited

A CIP catalogue record for this book is available from the British Library

A Library of Congress CIP catalogue record has been applied for

First published 2016

ISBN 9780117082854

Printed in the United Kingdom for The Stationery Office.
P002759920   c3   03/16

Contents

List of figures

List of tables

About this guide

Who's it for?

This guide is for anyone involved in planning who wants to improve their project performance.

If you are involved in project delivery, you are probably thinking that everyone around you knows how to plan – except you. You may be a team member, a project manager, or even a senior project or programme manager, and somehow the whole planning techniques thing passed you by. Your experience tells you that estimates always seem to be wrong, and nobody else seems to estimate any better than you, so why bother?

The point is that is that bad planning wastes time and money. If you are a complete novice to planning, this guide is for you. As a senior project manager with all the main project management qualifications, you probably don't spend enough time on planning and this guide will remind you of some fundamental techniques to help improve your overall performance.

Why do you need it?

Good question. Extensive research through maturity assessments has shown that inconsistency and lack of planning techniques are major weaknesses in the way we deliver projects. Projects come in many different shapes and sizes and it is recognized that no one size will fit all. However, the steps outlined in this publication establish a number of core principles that can apply to all projects.

Organizations that have effective project planning have increased ability to change and improve their performance through:

- A consistent cycle that enables the business to remain in control of the project
- Improved and consistent information, which enables more informed decision-making about priorities
- Early identification and management of issues, which maximizes the chances of success
- A greater transparency about the true cost and risk associated with individual initiatives
- An ability to share experiences, develop a body of knowledge and learn from others
- Planning in outline for a whole project, and in detail stage by stage as we recognize the 'planning horizon'.

A consistent approach to the development of robust and reliable plans that enable projects to deliver to time, cost and specification will help your organization to be at the forefront of project management delivery effectiveness.

Who's it by?

Rod Sowden

Rod Sowden founded Aspire Europe in 2004 after leaving the BBC. It is an organization dedicated to improving organizations' programme management performance. In the last 10 years he has travelled the world working on assignments and lecturing on a variety of topics. He was the lead author on the 2011 edition of *Managing Successful Programmes* (MSP®), a role he also held for the 2007 edition. The MSP Survival Guide series of publications, which support individuals in key programme roles, have also been written by Rod.

He pioneered the development of maturity models to measure organizational performance, and was the lead author in 2008 for the Portfolio, Programme and Project Maturity Model (P3M3®) (co-lead author for the 2015 version). Overall, Rod has helped more than 150 different organizations to improve their portfolio, programme, project and change management performance.

How is it organized?

Ideally this publication should be read before the idea for a project has arisen; however, we understand that in the real world planning is often not considered until after a project has been initiated. This publication provides 'staged guidance', allowing you to develop your plan in a step-by-step manner.

Each chapter represents a new stage in the project planning lifecycle and starts with an overview that includes:

- **Explanation and context** The likely things happening during the stage being described and when they would be expected.

- **Inputs/activities/outputs** A description of the key activities that should take place during the stage – including the inputs (documents or information required to complete the activities) and the outputs (documents or information which are created as a result of the activity).

Each of the activities within the stage is then described in turn. Each activity may contain:

- **Technique** A suggested best-practice technique to complete the activity. We provide a detailed explanation of the technique and how to apply it.

- **Example** A demonstration of the technique using a worked example.

- **Advanced information**   Information that is more challenging, such as a statistical technique.

- **Tips**   Extra information to help you further – identified by the 'pen nib' icon.

We have used two main case studies: a simple one in Chapters 2 and 3 that covers the setting up of a training course, and a more complex case study in Chapter 4 about setting up a helpline, which enables us to use more complex techniques.

Each chapter finishes with a list of role responsibilities for that stage.

Two appendices are also provided. Appendix 1 summarizes the different plans that you may come across during project planning, while Appendix 2 provides a brief summary of how the techniques and examples given in the main text can be pulled together into the overall project plan.

Foreword

The project management community comes in for a great deal of unfair criticism, much of which stems from the way in which projects, both large and small, are destined to fail before they start because of poor planning. Sadly, a proposal's chances of becoming a live project often depend more on the level of authority of its backers than its value to the organization, with the result that organizations devote large amounts of resources, especially money, to poorly planned projects.

All too often project management then takes the blame. This is like being asked to win a race with no clear route and no finishing line. Planning, especially before the project starts, brings clarity. *A Practical Guide to Project Planning* lays out a sensible process for planning a project and evaluating proposals in a consistent manner, leading to a realistic decision about their worth.

Successful projects start with a clear plan describing timing, scope, budgets, measures of business success and an understanding of what project success will really look like. This publication supports this ideal and brings a logic to where and when techniques should be used that is missing from many other books. Recognizing the critical need for upfront investment in resources to give clear targets and timescales, this guide will help you to devise a project plan that will give the project team and the organization a fair chance of delivering success.

Geoff Reiss M.Phil, HFAPM
Principal of Geoff Reiss Ltd
Honorary fellow of the Association for Project Management
Founder of ProgM – the programme management special interest group
www.geoffreiss.com

Preface

To achieve great things, two things are needed: a plan, and not quite enough time. Leonard Bernstein

In the past 10 years, Aspire Europe has been involved in more than 150 maturity reviews using the P3M3 maturity standard, provided consultancy to some 200 organizations, and delivered training to around 3,000 people across the globe. The one astoundingly consistent fact that has come out of this is that most organizations are very poor at project planning, and this is a major constraining factor on their ability to deliver.

The industry is not helping itself. If you have a project manager who has one of the main qualifications from the Association for Project Management (APM), Project Management International (PMI), the International Project Management Association (IPMA) or PRINCE2®, the reality is that during the week of training they probably spent less than 15% of the time learning about planning – so the lack of good planning should not surprise us.

The majority of project methods and in-house handbooks fail to provide standards or guidance on what techniques to use. This publication started life as guidance for one of Aspire Europe's clients, but the more we delved into the subject, the bigger it became, and before long the foundations of *A Practical Guide to Project Planning* had been laid.

We have created a step-by-step approach to developing a plan that is aligned with the common stages in a project, we have explained the best-practice techniques simply and we have given you examples based on straightforward case studies. As the people who reviewed the publication noted, the guide goes beyond just planning, because planning and project management are inherently linked through the project lifecycle.

Whether you are new to project management or have qualifications in the subject, you will find something in this publication for you. It will help to demystify some of the common vocabulary so when people use the terms you will understand what they mean, rather than nodding sagely while being totally confused.

If you are looking for a practical guide to help improve your project planning and increase your ability to control the plan, this is the publication for you. No matter what framework you are using, planning is a key element essential to achieve success.

Acknowledgements

In addition to thanking all the reviewers listed below, the author and publisher would also like to thank Tom Ford of Aspire Europe for his editorial support in managing the development process and his technical contributions to the content throughout the project; Peter Johnson of Aspire Europe for his contributions to the first draft and alignment with PRINCE2; and Graham Skinner for his ideas on the original work concepts for Bristol City Council.

About the reviewers

James Arrowsmith

James Arrowsmith is currently working for Antalis Limited as project management office director and is responsible for managing the company's portfolio of more than 50 projects. James has a proven project management track record stretching back over 25 years. He originally qualified as an accountant in the early 1990s. James has carried out a variety of jobs within finance (including finance director) and initially specialized in the implementation of finance projects. He moved into general project management in 2003 and has subsequently implemented a variety of programmes and projects after supplementing his practical experience with formal PRINCE2 and MSP training.

Paula Bartram

Paula Bartram joined Boeing Defence UK Ltd in February 2013 and is responsible for the programme management office, reporting into the vice president and managing director, David Pitchforth. Paula ensures organizational accountability, a more consolidated view of decision-making, transparency and maintenance of standards across its UK defence programmes including Information Services, UK Rotorcraft Support and Training. Her role also ensures the embedding of programme and project management best practices through appropriate governance and training.

Richard Caton

Richard Caton is a programme and project manager at the London Borough of Hackney. He is lead facilitator for the public sector Project and Programme Management (PPM) Community of Practice, a best-practice online network of around 1,800 people, and is also chair of the London PPM Forum. He has previously reviewed several Cabinet Office PPM guides, including *Management of Portfolios* (MoP®), *Portfolio, Programme and Project Offices* (P3O®) and P3M3. Richard developed Hackney's project management approach including methodology, tools, training and performance monitoring and was instrumental in developing the Public Sector Programme Management Approach, a wiki-based methodology viewed over a million times. Richard led Hackney's London 2012 Day Job programme and currently manages the council's Transforming Day Care project.

Adrian Davis

Adrian Davis is a member of the Civil Service Project Delivery Profession, with expertise in project controls such as planning, scheduling and dependency management. A former head of profession for planning within the Home Office IT Portfolio, he is now the senior manager leading on developing planning capability in the Department of Energy and Climate Change. As the Departmental Planning Advisor, Adrian is in contact with those skilled and unskilled in project planning and scheduling on a regular basis. He is a proven coach and very knowledgeable about the challenges in making planning easy for those new to the discipline.

Ralph Howle

Ralph Howle is the Corporate Planning Manager at Devon & Somerset Fire & Rescue Service. He has worked on large projects including the first voluntary combination of two fire and rescue services and the South West Regional Control Centre. He has led the tailoring and implementation of programme and project management methodologies and systems so they are matched to need and organizational maturity. Ralph also specializes in organizational performance management including the development of business models and frameworks, organizational approaches to business planning and undertaking improvement reviews. He leads on public consultations for substantial changes. Ralph volunteers his time as chairman of a local sports club.

Peter Johnson

Peter Johnson has skills in PPM with experience in public and private sectors in the UK and internationally in the sponsorship, management, application and training management of PRINCE2 (he chaired the PRINCE2 change control board for the 2009 version). He has MSP and APM qualifications and carries out Gateway (peer) reviews. As a civil servant, Peter was responsible for the development of PPM skills in central government as part of the Office of Government Commerce. Peter now designs and delivers PPM courses for training organizations and is continuing to contribute to the development of the PPM profession, as a volunteer, within the APM.

Kevin Parker

Kevin Parker is a project management professional with more than two decades of experience in a variety of sectors including health, justice, policing and sport. The last eight years have been spent at UK Sport, an organization that provides strategic investment to enable the UK's Olympic and Paralympic sports and athletes to achieve their full medal-winning potential. A key role here was project managing the award-winning 'Mission 2012' process that helped sports on their way to unprecedented success at London 2012.

Lee Pundsack

Lee Pundsack is a project manager for Plymouth City Council, working within the Transformation portfolio. He has been working for the local authority for 15 years, initially with Environmental Services. He started on the 'shop floor' and worked his way up through to management. He began his project management career in 2014 and became a qualified PRINCE2 practitioner in the same year. Recently, Lee has been working on the Commercialization project, creating new income streams for the council.

1 Introduction

Planning is at the core of good project management. Competent and accurate planning does not happen by accident: it is developed by learning from experience, using the right techniques at the right time to develop the required information and then acting upon that information.

The plan evolves – or, more accurately, plans evolve as there is usually more than one of them – through a number of steps. Planning itself is not guesswork; rather, it is the systematic calculation of the time activities will take, how much they will cost and when they will be delivered. However, it does involve estimating, making assumptions and therefore taking risks.

By having a clearly defined plan, the project manager will remove ambiguity and be able to take informed decisions that are transparent to the project board and stakeholders, and will provide an auditable impact assessment of the options.

The Association for Project Management (APM) values planning because it:

- Enables (viable) options to be evaluated
- Helps obtain commitment
- Enables communications
- Enables monitoring and control
- Enables informed change
- Helps to align with 'standards'
- May be useful to answer any future queries
- Informs the customer to enable effective contracting
- Helps the implementing suppliers to meet time, cost, and quality requirements
- Informs the risk management process, enabling monitoring and control.

1.1 Guiding principles of planning

> *I keep six honest serving men*
> *(They taught me all I knew)*
> *Their names are What and Why and When*
> *And How and Where and Who.* Rudyard Kipling

The guiding principles of What? Why? When? How? Where? and Who? underpin effective planning, and should be considered by all project team members who are involved in developing the plan.

- **Why?** tells us the drivers for change – and is a key element of a business case.

- **What?** tells us the objectives, which help us decide which option(s) to take forward at a high level and the precise deliverables or outputs of the project. We need confidence that these outputs will lead to business outcomes that, in turn, result in the benefits that are explicit in the business case.

- **How?** tells us the approach that colours the content of the plans – that is, the strategies that underpin the planning process.

- **Who? When?** and **Where?** will influence the resources needed and the planning schedule.

1.1.1 A consistent approach for all projects

All projects should follow the same basic steps and use the tools and templates provided to ensure that there is consistency of approach to planning that improves the quality of the project delivery. Without consistency, improvements cannot be made as there will be no baseline from which to build up.

1.1.2 Transparency about obstacles

All projects face challenges in terms of deadlines that have to be met. They may also be challenged to accommodate realism, ambiguity about what is required and the technical and organizational change difficulties to be faced. Failure to acknowledge these challenges and ambiguities will reduce the likelihood of success, even if it does seem expedient in the short term to ignore them.

Projects often start to go wrong very early in their lifecycles. Many of the issues that cause delays or failures could and should have been foreseen, but are either underestimated or ignored. Robust planning requires these issues to be defined and understood. A change as simple as a delay to the start date will probably result in a change to the end date unless something unexpected or fortunate happens, or additional resources (costs) are applied.

1.1.3 Plans should be metrics-driven

All plans should have estimates and tolerances of time, cost and quality built into them. By using the tools provided and accessing the experiences of others, the accuracy of these estimates will improve, leading to better delivery of business solutions.

If execution of a plan takes longer than estimated, and there is slippage against the plan, that time can never be re-captured. Therefore, unless a change is made to deal with the slippage, the project will run late and probably cost more. This in turn means later delivery of benefits and has a compound effect on meeting the business case's benefits scheduled in the benefits plan.

As part of the development of the plan, there will be a point against which the plan is 'baselined' for time, cost and quality. This is when the plan is authorized, usually by a project sponsor. Beyond that point, all reporting on performance and progress will be against this baseline. This will enable greater visibility of performance and trends within individual projects.

1.1.4 Involve stakeholders in the development

One regular complaint from auditors of failed projects is that stakeholders have not been adequately engaged. Stakeholders will generally take two forms:

- Those who will be supporting and enabling the project through knowledge and effort (supporters or blockers)

- Those who will be receiving the outputs of the project (winners or losers).

Tip
Recent studies by the UK's National Audit Office have shown that stakeholder involvement and perception are as significant to the success of a project as time, cost and quality management.

Stakeholders may well view the project as an inconvenient change or demand on their time, so they will need to be involved in the process of planning to minimize the impact on them and maximize the benefits of their involvement. Later these same stakeholders may be involved in many aspects of testing or quality control.

Nothing is for free. Stakeholder time and effort has a cost, whether it is financially attributable or intangible (e.g. time spent not undertaking other work or on trying to improve the stakeholder perception of the project). 'User' involvement needs to be budgeted for in plans – and committed to by a business representative when detailed plans are authorized.

1.1.5 Change must be controlled

A major reason for project failures is that during their lifetime changes to requirements and scope are included without any sort of impact assessment – on time, cost and quality or on the business case. Changes to requirements or time, cost and quality will require re-calculation of the estimates, the plan's costs and the business case.

Major changes should be analysed. However, in real life consideration is rarely given to actually stopping the project; generally the focus is on maintaining momentum and overcoming the obstacle rather than reviewing the overall viability of the project. When planning the governance (i.e. the project strategies) the project manager should propose the levels and scope of change authorities, and propose a change budget, in addition to the project budget and any financial tolerances.

Never underestimate the impact of the accumulation of the minor changes that go relatively unnoticed, without formal analysis and approval. It is the failure to control these small changes, as well as major ones, that often leads to time and cost overruns.

1.2 Project roles in planning

We refer to a variety of roles in this guide, and Table 1.1 provides a quick overview of what they do. At the end of each chapter, we give a summary of their role in the context of that particular stage.

Table 1.1 Overview of roles and responsibilities in project planning

Role	Responsibilities
Project sponsor	Person at the top of the project, personally responsible for making it a success, rarely from a professional project background but should have business seniority. PRINCE2 uses the term 'project executive', while others use 'sponsor'.
Project manager	Person responsible for getting things done, planning, organizing and managing resources and facilities that have been made available.
Business representative	Person who is the customer for the project at a junior level to the project sponsor. They have a very important role at the start to ensure the requirements are right and at the end because they will support the transition into service. In between they provide advice and support decisions about the functionality and transition. PRINCE2 has the term 'senior user' for this role, while others use 'customer'.
Suppliers (internal or external)	Persons representing the suppliers, who may be providing the services or outputs that are being built or acquired. PRINCE2 uses the term 'senior suppliers', while others use 'suppliers'.
Project management office/centre of excellence	In a larger organization, a central group that supports others or sets standards for how the project should be managed. It is sometimes also called a corporate portfolio office.

1.3 Stages of planning

Planning is an unnatural process; it is much more fun to do something. And the nicest thing about not planning is that failure comes as a complete surprise, rather than being preceded by a period of worry and depression.
Sir John Harvey Jones

Figure 1.1 illustrates the four main stages of planning.

Figure 1.1 The four main stages of planning

1.3.1 Defining the Plan

Once the project is authorized to move forward, based on business and benefits analysis, the first stage for the project team is to formalize requirements. This work will endeavour to remove ambiguity and ensure the intent of the project is understood.

This is often the stage that is skipped or has inadequate focus, and may be the source of trouble once the project moves into delivery.

In PRINCE2 this stage is often referred to as 'pre-project' and it is assumed it has been done. If this is not the case, this may be the source of problems that are experienced later.

1.3.2 Designing the Plan

At the outset of a project a detailed set of requirements may be handed over to the project manager by the business representative who has been developing the requirements. The extent and complexity of these requirements will be a key consideration in Designing the Plan.

A key element of Designing the Plan will be setting the scope for the project that will define the boundaries within which the planning will work.

All projects are, to some degree, unique. Therefore, the approach to Designing the Plan may need to vary. There are a variety of techniques that can be used and this stage will look at business options, previous experience (i.e. learning lessons from the past) and other techniques to gather together the information that will be used to develop the plan using a chosen approach.

This aligns loosely with Starting up a Project in PRINCE2.

1.3.3 Developing the Plan

Next, we take the information gathered during Designing the Plan and look to develop the plans matching the optimized delivery option and approach for the project. There could be many different types of plan to be developed, not just one.

This is the point where a number of techniques and processes are used to manage the complexity.

This aligns with the Initiating a Project stage in PRINCE2, where the project initiation documentation and plans are being created.

1.3.4 Delivering the Plan

If a plan is not monitored and controlled it cannot, realistically, result in delivery of the tested, approved and accepted outputs. That does not mean that a plan cannot change, but any changes should happen based on careful consideration of the implications. Projects will probably face a number of pitfalls. Many of these can be forecasted, and the control of the plan should include the navigation of these obstacles. The project manager can trade off any tolerances for time, cost and quality to maintain overall progress within stage tolerance (i.e. take corrective action), but will have to escalate forecasts of exceeding tolerances to the project sponsor.

This aligns with the Managing a Stage Boundary process within PRINCE2, where the outputs are being delivered.

Reviewing the plan is an essential part of delivery. There should be regular reviews for effectiveness and the lessons documented and learned. If this is not done then the same mistakes may be made again and again (as happens all too frequently in reality), so this is a key part of project planning.

This links to the Managing Product Delivery process within PRINCE2, where lessons are being learned about the effectiveness of planning.

1.4 Planning process overview

In this section we describe the main steps that need to be followed to deliver some or all aspects of the project.

Planning is a process that continues throughout the life of a project. The plan is not something that is created at the start of the project and then left to gather dust on a shelf – it is at the heart of good project management. Without a plan, a project will become a set of random activities that might produce something of value at some stage; equally it may not.

The project should be commissioned in response to a business driver, whether it is a threat or an opportunity that has been identified. Within your organization this may trigger business analysis work to develop understanding of the driver and the likely effects it will have on the business operations. Business benefits derived from the analysis should be the justification for the investment in the project.

Once the analysis has been done, one or more objectives can be set, and these will set the direction and scope of the project. A well-structured project will also have success criteria defined at the start, normally linked to the objectives.

The next step is to establish the requirements, but this is an area that is often overlooked. If you do not have a clear understanding of what the project is required to deliver, what chances are there of being successful? The requirements set out what the organization needs from the project to enable it to achieve the outcomes and benefits.

Once the requirements have been defined, the next step is to produce a technical specification of what is required to be produced (referred to as 'outputs' or 'deliverables'). Outputs, known as 'products' in PRINCE2, are the anticipated results of the project. An output can be anything that is tangible: a report, a policy, a building, or an item of technology. The product description describes how the requirements will be met, and what the output will look like. We use the term 'product description' here, but it could also be called a technical specification.

Creating the output as part of delivery usually constitutes the main part of the project. The output may be created in-house or procured in some other way, dependent on what it is. Delivery will normally be made up of a number of steps. Each step provides a control point for decisions to continue or change direction. A step may be linked to the creation of individual outputs or groups of outputs; this will depend on the project.

On completion, the output is tested and ready for use. In project-speak this is 'completed output' and is also an output of the project work. An example might be a database that has been created, tested and can be used when the other elements of the project such as training of staff on the new database are completed.

There will come a point where all project outputs have been completed and are ready to move into live use. At this point the organization has the capability to do something new or something different. Circumstances can change, so the organization can actually choose not to go ahead and could even mothball the outputs. Hence, this state is referred to as 'capability'. An example might be when an IT system is tested and ready to go, and everyone has been trained, but due to unforeseen problems with something else the live date is postponed.

From a project perspective, the final state is likely to be the outcome. This is the point after transition has been delivered and the capability is now live. The new capability and maybe the new ways of working are in place, the business has changed the way it delivers its services and it is now stable again.

Benefits will follow, but these will be within the domain of the business areas themselves and normally outside the scope of the project team. However, decisions during the project will be driven by benefits and it should always be remembered that the project exists only because of identified benefits.

2 Defining the Plan

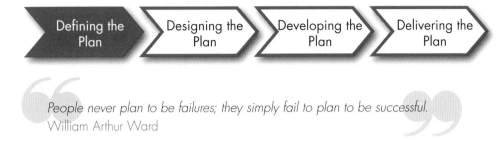

Projects exist to satisfy some sort of need. The term used to describe that need is 'requirements' (i.e. what we want the project to deliver). The requirements then inform the objectives and everything else that follows.

Surprisingly, getting the requirements properly defined is often difficult, and the lack of them is often the cause of problems. If people have not committed to paper what they require then assumptions have to be made, and during the development and delivery people change their minds, resulting in delays and disputes.

The inputs to this first stage may have already been created by the time the project team begin their work, but there may be other documentation (as listed in the inputs in Figure 2.1) that will need to be reviewed to gather information that will help with this stage.

Before you go any further, try to find examples of where projects like yours have been undertaken within your organization or in other organizations, as there may be valuable information about the challenges you might face that you need to plan for.

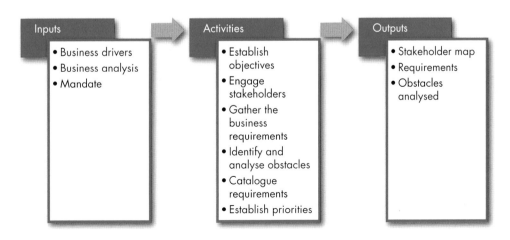

Figure 2.1 Inputs, activities and outputs of Defining the Plan

A stakeholder map is a key output of this stage, as it will help everyone to understand the impact and priorities of different individuals and groups.

You should compile detailed requirements, which will be the single source of information that can be consulted to understand what the business expects the project to deliver. It is quite likely that more detailed work will need to be undertaken to develop technical or functional specifications to support the achievement of the requirements, and different disciplines will approach this work using their own best practice (e.g. IT or construction).

You will also have identified and analysed the constraints, most likely recorded in a risk or issue log of some sort.

In this chapter we use a simple example of setting up a project planning training course to illustrate the techniques and how they might be applied.

2.1 Establish objectives

At the outset of the project there is often ambiguity about what is going to be achieved, and working to clear the ambiguity is a key aspect of the project early in the lifecycle. This will require engagement at a number of levels.

The project sponsor will need to clarify the strategic context and constraints within which the project should deliver. These will provide the top-level objectives resulting from the discussions with the stakeholders.

Among all the information it is sometimes easy to lose sight of the project's purpose, so it is often helpful to have some simple statement, sometimes called a charter, vision or mission. For example:

'The aim is to improve the quality of our project planning in order to increase the levels of successful delivery and reduce the unwanted costs of project delay.'

Tip
If the project is part of a programme, the requirements should be linked to the programme blueprint, which defines the capability required or provides the full details.

Objectives can come from many sources but the following can be used as a guide to categorization:

● **Strategic objectives** The objectives that drive the need for the project. They may be linked to the corporate objectives, meet a legislative requirement, deal with service weaknesses, or be in response to competitor behaviour or a policy decision that needs to be implemented. Work to define the benefits of these objectives may already have been undertaken and should be captured.

- **Operational objectives** These are objectives that are driving the business need for the project at an operational level. They are likely to reflect the need for greater efficiency or to improve the quality of services that are being delivered. The objectives may have been defined as part of the development of the benefits, so there may be specific objectives that the operations function will need to meet to satisfy the benefit.

- **Project objectives** These objectives are linked to the internal performance of the project or are specific to the way the project will operate (e.g. in the way that it approaches the development of options or manages a major obstacle). Other project objectives should reflect the compliance with corporate standards and how the project will achieve effective delivery. Projects are often assessed against delivery performance to targets for time, cost and quality – often extended to include delivery of scope within risk tolerance, modified by sensitivity to benefits in the business case.

Many projects appear to fail because this holistic view of what is required has not been captured through the objectives.

Projects can be successful in terms of delivering to time, cost and quality constraints, but then fail due to poor transition into the business. A few examples are given in the list below:

- The Channel Tunnel ended up with excessive expenses but was an operational success

- The Wembley Stadium project was late and over budget, but the objective of an excellent venue for English football was achieved

- The building of Heathrow Terminal 5 was a huge project success that failed to be implemented into service as intended, resulting in enormous damage to the reputation of BA and Heathrow Airport Holdings Limited.

Projects, like organizations, do not exist in isolation from the real world where there is a constantly changing environment. The project team cannot control events, but it should be aware of changes that may affect its ability to deliver. The word PESTLE is often used as a reminder of external factors to consider:

- **Political** Internal politics within your organization as well as local and national politics

- **Economic** The state of local, national or international economies and markets that you operate in

- **Societal** Trends in society that may affect your project in terms of attitudes and priorities

- **Technological** Advances that could render your project redundant or offer opportunities that you had not expected

- **Legislative** Changes to your sector or markets that may affect your project or organization positively or negatively

- **Environmental** Impact of changes on the environment in which you operate.

As an example, at the start of 2015, a major reduction in oil price (driven by economic downturn globally, and oversupply of oil, partially due to unrest in the Middle East and between Russia and Ukraine) led to the cancellation of significant capital projects within the oil industry but provided opportunities for companies in terms of reduction in transportation costs.

2.1.1 Technique

Weak, ambiguous or unrealistic objectives will set unrealistic expectations of what can be achieved by the project, the business operations or the organization. Therefore, they should not be subjective. Ideally, objectives should also be SMART:

- **S**pecific to the project
- **M**easurable to prove success
- **A**chievable, as agreed with key stakeholders and within the ability of the project to deliver
- **R**ealistic in the context of the time and budget available
- **T**ime-bound so that specified expectations of when results are achieved are met.

To capture and confirm the objectives for the project, use a table that includes columns for the objective and its description, together with date, owner, type and measure.

2.1.2 Example

Table 2.1 is a simple example of each type of objective and how it might be measured for the training course being envisaged. Such a table will provide solid direction on which to base your project and identify what your plan will need to achieve.

2.2 Engage stakeholders

As part of establishing the objectives, you should have been able to identify the main groups and individuals who will initially be part of the project and involved with establishing requirements.

Firstly, stakeholder analysis should answer the following questions:

- Who are the stakeholders and how should we group them? Perhaps they fall into groups such as those in change governance, those who will be the users who will eventually accrue the benefits, and those who may be suppliers and influencers, such as the media or lobby groups.
- How does the change affect them and what do they need to know? They may be victims or beneficiaries (winners or losers).
- Are they supporters or opponents of the change (supporters or blockers)?

Table 2.1 Examples of objectives for the training course project

Objective	Description	Date	Owner	Type	Measure
Improve the quality of planning across the organization	It is necessary to raise the performance of the project delivery to avoid the delays and losses resulting from poor planning	End	Project sponsor	Strategic	Independent assurance that the service meets the legislative requirements. Grants being delivered.
Deliver the training with minimum business disruption	Staff will have no more than one day out of the office and training will be supported by self-learning	End	Business representative	Operational	Number of people gaining a formal qualification. Productivity loss.
Comply with organization project lifecycle controls	The project will comply with the standards, reporting and stage gates	End	Project manager	Project	Assurance review by independent group. Post (end) project review and lessons learned. Audit trail of gate/peer reviews.

Once this information has been gathered the communications planning can take place. Different individuals and groups will be at different stages of awareness about the change. Therefore your communications will need to take them through the stages shown in Table 2.2 as necessary.

Tip
One of the biggest obstacles that a project can face is a lack of willingness to engage. You therefore need to focus communications on trying to answer the question 'What is in it for you?'.

2.2.1 Technique

The technique for engaging stakeholders is based on market segmentation and understanding the relationship between customer groups and products. It is a very powerful 'at a glance' view of the stakeholder environment.

Table 2.2 Communications stages

Stage	Status
Awareness	Make them aware that a change is happening, that it will affect them in some way and that there is something in it for them.
Interest	Build on initial awareness enough for them to be willing to do some research, reply to emails, respond to calls or agree to have a meeting or attend an event.
Engagement	Exploit interest to the point where two-way dialogue can take place, information is being exchanged and views are being developed.
Commitment	Once constructive dialogue has taken place a stakeholder will be in a position to decide whether they support the change or not. It may be that they still oppose the change, but at least they will have made that decision based on evidence and consideration rather than a knee-jerk reaction. Good stakeholder engagement will look to find ways of moving people from blocker towards supporter, perhaps by identifying some (small/tactical) benefit that supports the blockers' broader agendas.

The stakeholder map is a matrix where the stakeholders are recorded and their relationship with the major changes is illustrated. There are many ways to enhance the map with additional information in the cells, including colour coding, comments etc.

The map should be maintained as part of the normal management information and changes should be tracked as part of the communications plan.

The technique is also used to work out which power/importance area stakeholders occupy and what communications are appropriate, as listed below:

● **Very high power/very high importance** For these stakeholders face-to-face (1:1) conversations will be worthwhile.

● **High power/high importance** These stakeholders will benefit from active consultation (one to many) such as questionnaires, focus groups or workshops.

● **Medium power/medium importance** For these stakeholders more passive consultation (one to many) such as presentations supplemented by question-and-answer sessions may be appropriate.

● **Low power/low importance** Here communication is either by telling/broadcasting ('pushing') information or relies on stakeholders 'pulling' information from physical or virtual notice boards.

Once you have established the appropriate communications with the stakeholders, there are three main techniques that you can apply for gathering information. These are:

● **Questionnaires** This is a good way of gathering general information and views about what is required.

- **Workshops** These can be used to consolidate information, views and opinions and to solve problems.

- **One-to-one interviews** Such interviews are very useful for extracting specific information and dealing with stakeholders who are more sensitive, have overriding priorities or may need persuasion to provide support.

2.2.2 Example

The matrix in Table 2.3 shows the levels of support of each group of stakeholders for the objectives of the example training course project.

Table 2.3 Stakeholder support for the training course project's objectives

	Objective 1	Objective 2	Objective 3
Course delegates			
Learning and development department			
Senior managers			
Course supplier			
Venue owners			

Key ■ = resistors; ■ = ambivalent; ■ = supporter.

From this kind of matrix you can quickly see the objectives of the project which are popular and unpopular with different groups, and this will help you develop your communications plan and understand the level of risk being faced.

2.3 Gather the business requirements

Requirements management is concerned with meeting the needs of end-users through identifying and specifying what they need.

Requirements may be focused on outcomes (e.g. describing what people should be able to do as a result of commissioning a new building), where the main concern is to describe what is wanted rather than how it should be delivered. Alternatively, requirements may need to be specified in precise terms (e.g. when ordering a technical component to fit with existing office machinery). Requirements may be described in any way between these two extremes. The important issue is that those specifying the requirement have an adequate understanding of what the users need and how the market is likely to meet that need. Requirements need to be expressed in a way that keeps any likely changes to a minimum. Changes to requirements once the project moves into delivery can have major impacts on scope, cost and timescale and are one of the major causes of project failure.

Establishing the requirements is a process in itself. Initially there may be much ambiguity and, wherever possible, this ambiguity should be removed. There is a tendency to rush this activity; however, if there is not clarity about what needs to be produced, what hope is there of delivering it? Ambiguity in requirements is often the source of failure in projects.

2.3.1 Technique

In order to specify business requirements the following should be considered:

- **Context** The organizational setting in which the requirements are emerging. It should be recognized that all requirements have attributes that are a rich source of management information. Each project should select the attributes that are critical to its success (e.g. customer benefit, effort, development priority etc.).

- **Requirements** This includes understanding the boundaries, determining the stakeholders, recognizing goals, using scenarios, investigating feasibility and understanding risks.

- **Modelling and analysis** Understanding the effects of the changes at different levels of the organization.

- **Communications** Use of appropriate language, documentation and other illustrations to maintain appropriate two-way dialogue (i.e. consultation) and understanding with stakeholders. Also ensuring that requirements are traceable.

- **Gaining agreements** Validation, negotiation, conflict resolution and prioritization of requirements.

- **Evolution** Ensuring that the solution to meeting the requirements is responsive to environmental change and that any changes in requirements can be managed and controlled effectively (involves impact analysis and configuration management).

When we have defined the objectives and understand which stakeholders are interested in what, we need to bring all the information together so that the extent of what the project will need to deliver is understood. Requirements are basically the business changes that the project will need to deliver.

At this point, the requirements may take a variety of forms, from a specific (objective) technical requirement through to an evolving expectation. The key thing is to capture all the requirements, as they will shape what stakeholders are expecting and will need to be included or excluded from the scope of the project in the next stage.

There is a danger that requirements are driven by the features of a supplier's products, so care needs to be taken to differentiate (as obstacles) such requirements when they arise, as these will affect the options for delivering the solution.

At the end of this activity a document detailing business requirements should be produced. This needs to capture the following information:

- **Reference** Unique ID for the requirement

- **Requirement** Description of the requirement

- **Business impact** The effect of having this requirement or facility

- **Originator** The person or group who requested the requirement

- **Objective(s) served** There should be a link between the requirement and the objectives.

2.3.2 Example

The clearest way to document the business requirements is probably by using a table, as shown in Table 2.4 (based on the training course project). Such a table gives an overview of what the project is required to deliver and how it aligns with business objectives.

Table 2.4 Requirements of the training course project

Ref	Requirement	Business impact	Originator	Objective(s) served
001	All courses to be held in central training facilities	Minimize loss of staff from business and avoid costs of travel	Tom	Deliver the training with minimum business disruption
002	Course must be supported by detailed guidance	Will enable reference to the materials after the course is completed, so the course will have more effect	Rod	Improve the quality of planning across the organization
003	Course must be concluded within 1 day	This will reduce resistance from line managers to releasing staff	Alice	Deliver the training with minimum business disruption

2.4 Identify and analyse obstacles

There will almost inevitably be obstacles that the project will need to overcome to achieve its goals. The sooner these are identified, recognized and understood the better, as this will help to set expectations of what can be achieved at a reasonable level.

'Obstacle' is a generic term that, in this context, identifies anything that could get in the way of delivery. Obstacles could include hard deadlines, costs, problems, supply chain difficulties, organizational standards, dependencies and assumptions that are being made about the capability of your organization to deliver this project.

As all projects are unique in some way, there are likely to be obstacles that are individual to the project. The main aim is to document the things that could get in the way of success.

2.4.1 Technique

The main techniques for handling obstacles are techniques for issue management (where there are known problems) or techniques for risk management (where there are problems that might occur). To start with it is helpful not to be too concerned about what type of obstacle it is, but to make sure that the obstacle is recorded and the potential understood.

The following is a checklist for identifying obstacles:

- **Lessons** Has your organization undertaken a similar project in the past? If not, are you aware of a comparable organization (a reference site) that has?
- **Deadlines** Are there deadlines that must be met and cannot be moved?
- **Costs** What expectations have been set on the costs? Is there a defined budget in place or money set aside?
- **Resources (capability and capacity)** Are there suitable and sufficient resources available in-house to do this? (The resources may be committed elsewhere – or just not there.)
- **Priority** What level of priority does this project have against other initiatives current or planned?
- **Stakeholders** Are the majority of stakeholders supportive? How powerful are the blockers?
- **Problems** Are there any known technical problems that may obstruct the projects?
- **Dependencies** Are there any external dependencies on other initiatives that could undermine success?
- **Prerequisites** Are there any outstanding decisions needed either inside or outside the organization?
- **Supply chain** What is the level of dependency on partners (private or public sector) delivering a significant component of the work?
- **Change context** If the project is part of a programme, what issues or risks will affect this project?

A workshop of key individuals within the project (including stakeholders and sponsors) is a very good technique for reviewing the checklist and identifying potential obstacles; however, this can be expensive in terms of management time. Speaking to people individually and researching similar projects is an alternative approach.

As mentioned earlier, there is a danger that people get distracted by considering whether an obstacle is a risk, an issue or something else, so while drawing up a list of obstacles just try to identify the challenges that could be faced or the problems you already know you need to resolve.

Once all the challenges and problems have been identified, then they need to be carefully reviewed to decide whether they are:

● A threat

● An opportunity

● An issue

● An event that triggers a threat or opportunity

● A consequence of a threat or opportunity.

If it exists, the organization's guidance on risk and issue management should be used.

Tip
Focus on the cause of a threat, as this will keep the number of risks down to a manageable amount. It is common to find risk registers overloaded with items that are not actual risks, but events that could trigger a threat or opportunity or the consequence of a threat or opportunity.

2.4.2 Example

Most organizations have a standard approach to managing issues and risks. If not, a simple log, as shown in Table 2.5, would probably suffice. The log should include:

● **Obstacle** What is the potential problem?

● **Effect** What will be the effect on the plan?

● **Owner** Who is the person responsible for dealing with it?

● **Type** What type of obstacle do you think it is?

Maintaining a log will help to moderate expectations as part of the planning process. It is the lack of visibility of obstacles that leads to optimistic bias in planning.

Table 2.5 Log of possible obstacles to the training course project

Obstacle	Effect	Owner	Type
Local managers may resist releasing staff to attend training	Course places will not be used up. Improvements will not be achieved.	Sponsor	Resourcing

To manage obstacles there are two approaches:

● Make someone responsible to resolve the obstacle

● Collectively assess the most likely scenario and develop plans around this.

2.5 Catalogue requirements

During information gathering it is highly likely that you will come across conflicting requirements or those that are described differently but may be the same. It is also distinctly possible that requirements being fed into your project may also have been given to other projects. It is therefore useful to categorize the information to enable analysis and comparison. Different projects will have different requirements. However, a standard organizational approach is required to ensure consistency.

At this point the priority is to capture the requirements rather than make decisions about the feasibility of delivering them. Early in the project lifecycle some requirements may look unrealistic or unachievable, but may become feasible later, or there may be another project that can pick them up at some stage. Similarly, requirements that look straightforward may hide complexity or innovations that are yet to be understood, and until that information is available requirements should be simply catalogued.

Requirements will need some sort of business change to happen. This may be to create, amend or remove some service or related aspects.

2.5.1 Technique

It is important to establish some criteria for cataloguing, sorting and filtering requirements to enable us to have different views of the requirements through a common syntax. There are many criteria that could be used. Here are some standard categories:

- **Accommodation** (AC) Changes to or provision of accommodation or other related facilities management services
- **Business process** (BP) Development or change to a business process
- **Human resources** (HR) Changes to structures, skills or numbers of staff
- **IT software** (ITS) Changes to or provision of IT software
- **IT hardware** (ITH) Changes to or provision of IT hardware
- **Statutory** (ST) Change that is needed to meet a legal requirement
- **Web** (WB) Changes to or provision of internal or external information via the internet
- **Policy** (PO) Change that is needed to an organization's policy
- **Training** (TR) Provision of a training service
- **Reporting** (RP) Development of reporting or changes to the way information is presented
- **Supply chain** (SC) Establishing or delivering changes to the way services are procured
- **Construction** (CO) Change that requires building of new facilities
- **Telecoms** (TP) Provision of or changes to telephony, telecoms or voice and data-related services.

2.5.2 Example

The requirements category can be added to the basic requirements shown in Table 2.4. Table 2.6 shows this for the example of the training course project.

For more complex requirements it will be necessary to have multiple categories for each, and in that case a table such as the one shown in Table 2.7 may suffice, with each category being given a column.

Table 2.6 Requirements and categories for the training course project

Ref.	Requirement	Business impact	Originator	Objective served	Category
001	All courses to be held in central training facilities	Minimize loss of staff from business and avoid costs of travel	Tom	Deliver the training with minimum business disruption	TR
002	Course must be supported by detailed guidance	Will enable reference to the materials after the course is completed, so the course will have more effect	Rod	Improve the quality of planning across the organization	BP
003	Course must be concluded within 1 day	This will reduce resistance from line managers to releasing staff	Alice	Deliver the training with minimum business disruption	HR

Table 2.7 Example of requirements with multiple categories

Ref	Requirement	BP	CO	HR	ITH	ITS	TP	TR	WB
002	Course must be supported by detailed guidance	X		X		X		X	

Once the requirements have been established they should be agreed with the stakeholders. This will require a second round of communications to ensure that the requirements have been correctly understood and captured.

2.6 Establish priorities

As well as checking requirements, it is important to establish priorities. Not all requirements will have equal priority and a structured approach to decision-making will be needed. Stakeholders will have their own views on what is important, and not all will be satisfied.

2.6.1 Technique

The best way to check the requirements is to distribute the table of requirements (e.g. Table 2.6) and request that the stakeholders confirm them. As part of this process, you should also establish the priority of each of the requirements for the various stakeholder groups. All ratings should be on a scale of 1 to 5, with 1 as highest. Thus:

- High 1
- Medium high 2
- Medium 3
- Medium low 4
- Low 5.

In establishing the priority of the requirements for various groups, you are looking to find the common priorities. Criteria for priority rating are:

- **Level of support** This indicates requirements that are important to most stakeholders and those that are isolated and important to only one group. Filtering by originator will show which stakeholder group proposed the requirement, but we can enhance this by a more thorough stakeholder analysis leading to a detailed stakeholder profile showing degree of support and 'winners'.

- **Level of priority** How important are the requirements in terms of priority? This will require stakeholders to rate the importance on a scale.

- **Level of importance** How important is the requirement to meeting the objectives of the project? If it directly contributes to the achievement of more than one objective, then it should be rated more highly.

- **Level of complexity** How easy it is for the project to deliver may also have a bearing. If the requirement can be met by a relatively simple change or as part of other work then it may represent a quick win which will help to keep the stakeholders on board.

Tip
A common technique for prioritizing the level of importance of requirements is known as 'MoSCoW'. This categorizes the needs in terms of 'Must haves', 'Should haves', 'Could haves' and 'Would like but won't get' as a means of prioritizing various needs.

2.6.2 Example

Once the priority criteria have been rated, the requirements can be analysed in a number of different ways by using comparison matrices with different criteria on the axis. Table 2.8 provides an example of what should be recorded as a minimum.

Table 2.8 Analysis of the requirements for the training course project

Requirement	Support	Priority	Importance	Complexity	Total rating
001	1	1	1	4	6
002	2	2	2	4	10
003	1	2	1	1	5

By recording the scores in this way you can quickly see how the requirements should be prioritized; the requirement with the lowest total rating is the highest priority. In a complex project, some weighting may be needed to ensure that the requirements that have the highest business importance are dealt with as highest priority. In many instances you may need also to give a weighting to priority and importance but this moves use into the realms of business analysis techniques.

Table 2.9 shows the requirements as set out in Table 2.6, with overall priority levels attached.

Table 2.9 Requirements and priorities for the training course project

Ref	Requirement	Business impact	Originator	Objective served	Category	Priority
001	All courses to be held in central training facilities	Minimize loss of staff from business and avoid costs of travel	Tom	Deliver the training with minimum business disruption	TR	1
002	Course must be supported by detailed guidance	Will enable reference to the materials after the course is completed, so the course will have more effect	Rod	Improve the quality of planning across the organization	BP	3
003	Course must be concluded within 1 day	This will reduce resistance from line managers to releasing staff	Alice	Deliver the training with minimum business disruption	TR	2

2.7 Role responsibilities for Defining the Plan

The role responsibilities for this stage can be summarized as follows:

- **Project sponsor**
    - Ensuring that requirements are gathered using a robust approach
    - Ensuring that there is appropriate alignment between the project objectives and the prioritized requirements
    - Taking a lead in bringing clarity to what is required from the project

- **Project manager**
    - Managing the process of requirements gathering
    - Establishing any weighting criteria to support requirements prioritization
    - Stakeholder engagement and communications planning
    - Maintaining information and audit trails
    - Establishing and delivering workshops where appropriate

- **Business representative**
    - Ensuring that the requirements defined meet the needs of the business areas
    - Organizing suitable business resources to contribute to the identification of requirements
    - Reviewing and validating the prioritization of the requirements

- **Supplier (internal or external)**
    - Providing advice and input on the ability of the market to deliver the requirements
    - Providing technical advice and comments on the feasibility and ease of provision of the requirements

- **Project management office/centre of excellence**
    - Advising on other projects that may be generating similar requirements
    - Advising on the use of planning frameworks and techniques
    - Identifying cross-project dependencies and opportunities to remove or exploit, in order to gain efficiencies
    - Acting as a central repository for project information.

3 Designing the Plan

As described in Chapter 1, plans can be viewed as documents that should cover the why, what, how, who, when and where of project delivery. During the Defining the Plan stage we should have clarified 'why' and an element of the 'what' in the business objectives and requirements, so we are now going to take the steps to expand on the 'what' and develop our understanding of 'how'.

Figure 3.1 shows the inputs, activities and outputs of the Designing the Plan stage, and Table 3.1 provides an overview of the tools used.

3.1 Map the journey

In the early days of the project, the information available will probably be inadequate to formalize the plan. There is also a danger that the project team moves too quickly to producing plans, which focus too much on details rather than the overall, high-level view of the journey. Therefore at the start of this stage it is useful to 'map' the journey. A graphical representation will make communications with non-technical stakeholders easier and provide a valuable input into identifying the milestones and control points for the project.

Tip
Do not be surprised if this step highlights areas of concern relating to scope. It may well be the case that things need to happen which were not spotted earlier.

Figure 3.1 Inputs, activities and outputs of Designing the Plan

Table 3.1 Overview of the tools used in Designing the Plan

Activity	Tool
Map the journey	Outcome modelling
Identify outputs	Hierarchical structures or mind maps
	Product breakdown structure
Product sequencing	Product sequence diagram
Develop specifications	Product descriptions

3.1.1 Technique

Outcome modelling produces a simple diagrammatic illustration of what needs to be achieved. It provides an overview of how the requirements fit into the bigger scheme of things and how the objectives will be met by the project.

As we develop our plans, we will become more specific about whether it is a product, activity, output or outcome that is being mapped; however, at this stage we just want to illustrate at a very high level what has to happen.

Tip
Sticky notes and a wall are a great way to model outcome – create a note for each of the things you need to achieve and try to put them in some sort of order.

3.1.2 Example

An outcome model for the project training course example used earlier shows what needs to be done to organize a course (see Figure 3.2).

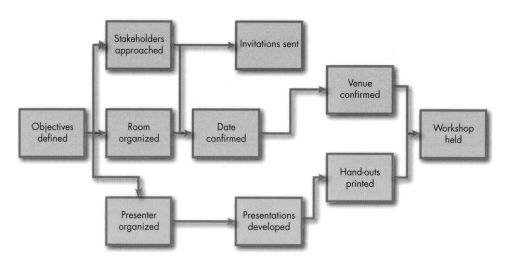

Figure 3.2 Outcome model for training course project

The objectives need to be defined before anything else can happen. This is followed by finding a room, inviting the stakeholders and booking a presenter. Some outcomes in the sequence enable one or more other outcomes whereas others are self-fulfilling in their own right. Where other outcomes are enabled, the following outcomes are 'dependent' on the earlier outcomes, so the term 'dependencies' is used a lot in project planning.

An outcome model can be very helpful for explaining the project to people not very familiar with project management. The illustration also shows how some outcomes are more critical than others because they have more dependencies.

3.2 Identify outputs

As we move further into the detail of Designing the Plan, some of the challenges we face will be of increasing complexity. Figure 3.3 shows the sequence model for defining this part of the journey.

Having developed the sequence model so that the journey is now defined, the next step is to work out what will need to be created and put into place to enable the journey.

You need to identify what products will be created and order them into a structure that can be used to plan timing, resourcing, dependencies and costs. Identifying and mapping outputs is often described as 'creating a product breakdown structure'.

Tip
Thinking about products focuses us on what we need to produce and deters us from jumping straight into building a 'to do' list of activities, which will result in a lack of focus.

This step is often easier for projects that deliver outputs such as buildings, computers, reports and other physical items that you can see, touch and use. It is not quite so straightforward for some 'softer' business projects; for example, changing a culture, providing an improved monitoring service for children at risk or improving customer perception. Part of the reason for this is that in business projects there are greater relationships between the component parts and they are often more difficult to define.

Figure 3.3 Sequence model for the identification of products

Tip
More complex projects will need more time to identify the outputs: however, time spent working on the specification increases your chances of achieving successful results. Failure to meet expectations is often due to a lack of detail in what is required.

If your project is delivering some sort of business change, you should consider the wider implications on the way it operates rather than just thinking about the functionality you need to provide; there are many examples of successful projects being a business failure.

When planning this sort of project the POTI model provides a wider view of the things you should consider. The POTI model can be summarized as follows:

- **P**rocess The processes you may need to build or contribute to.

- **O**rganization The people and the departments where changes will need to be delivered.

- **T**echnology The IT, accommodation, machinery and any other assets (e.g. vehicles) used to do the job. Think 'infrastructure'. You may be changing this.

- **I**nformation on performance The reporting that will be used to manage the quality and performance of the service (i.e. key performance indicators in the business rather than just project performance against time, costs and quality).

If your project is part of a programme, it should have a blueprint with which your project can be aligned. If your project is standalone and not part of a programme, the POTI model is useful in two respects:

- It can assist with checking the scope of the change that the project will deliver. Some new requirements may need to be added to the scope of the project as project tasks.

- It can be of use for the project board or steering group, in particular the business representative, to help them check whether all aspects of POTI will be addressed. If they are not all addressed, the implementation into service may fail.

Beware of making too many assumptions about the current state. Take time to find out how things work at present so that the gap to be filled by the project outputs is fully scoped and understood.

3.2.1 Technique

There are two techniques that are useful for identifying and mapping outputs (or creating a product breakdown structure). The first is mind mapping and the second is a hierarchical list of the components required to create an output.

Tip
A product breakdown structure can be expanded into a work breakdown structure to show tasks and an organizational breakdown structure to show what skills and resources will be needed.

A mind map is a diagram used to represent words, ideas, tasks, or other items linked to and arranged around a central key word or idea. It presents ideas in a radial, graphical and non-linear manner. Mind maps are used to generate, visualize, structure and classify ideas, and as an aid to studying and organizing information, solving problems, making decisions and writing. The mind map provides the basis for creating the hierarchical product breakdown structure, which shows the outputs of the project in a pecking order and puts more organization and formality around the relationships.

The process of defining the product breakdown structure will be iterative. As the work progresses you may discover areas for which you do not have requirements, or alternatives that will require consultation with the stakeholders.

For some people, the product-based planning approach is not natural. If this is the case for you, think about what needs to be in place and working, namely the outcomes, and work backwards to identify what needs to be in place. This is a good reason for using a mind map to start the process; once it has been created then more order and definition can be applied using a hierarchical product breakdown structure.

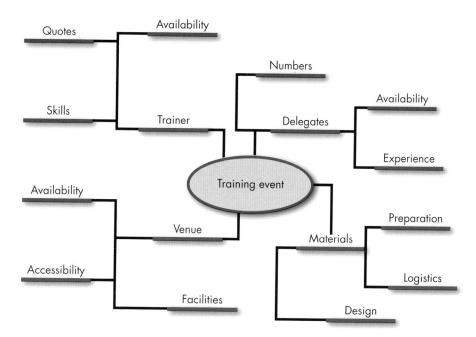

Figure 3.4 An example of a mind map for the training course project

The product breakdown structure should be communicated to stakeholders for their approval, although it may require some explanation to the uninitiated. It should be mandatory for all projects to produce a product breakdown structure.

3.2.2 Example 1 – a product breakdown structure in mind map format

Figure 3.4 is a mind map using the example of the training course project. Initially, it randomly captures the things that need to be sorted out. As it develops it can take more structure, but it is good to get the big headings down early as these tend to shape the later thinking. In a workshop sticky notes can be issued to create the map. If you are doing it as an individual, you might prefer to use computer software developed for mind mapping, flowcharts and diagramming, or presentations, to achieve the same effect.

3.2.3 Example 2 – a product breakdown structure in hierarchical format

It is relatively straightforward to change the format of a product breakdown structure from a mind map into a more hierarchical list by using the same main headings and breaking them down into specific products that need to be created (see Figure 3.5). The mind map is quite a random collection of ideas, while the hierarchical format of the product breakdown structure translates this into the specifics that the project will need to deliver and plan for.

Table 3.2 is an example of the breakdown structure for the materials required for the training course, as used in previous examples. It identifies the key component parts of the pre-course packs, delegate packs, hand-outs and materials (stationery) required by the trainer.

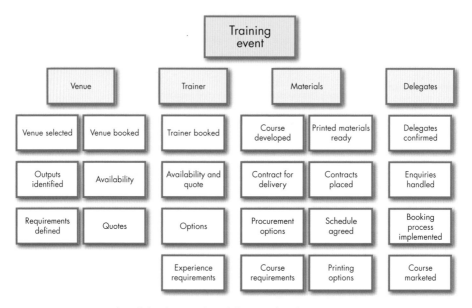

Figure 3.5 An example of the hierarchical format for the training course project

Table 3.2 Output 1 – Materials pack for the training course project

1 Materials pack			
1.1 Pre-course pack	1.2 Delegate pack	1.3 Hand-outs	1.4 Stationery
1.1.1 Email 1.1.2 Timetable 1.1.3 Workbook 1.1.4 Syllabus 1.1.5 Manual	1.2.1 Ring bind folder 1.2.2 Exam delegate guidance 1.2.3 Slides	1.3.1 Sample Paper 1 1.3.2 Sample Paper 2 1.3.3 Feedback form	1.4.1 Subject dividers 1.4.2 Pen 1.4.3 Pencil 1.4.4 A4 ruled pad

Tip
Using reference numbers for each element of the product breakdown structure will be helpful for allocating responsibilities and tasks and communicating issues.

The requirements for the materials informed and defined the specification, which was then used for the product description. At this stage though, we are able to break the materials down into a product breakdown structure of their own. Each of the elements described would have their own unique definition. It is important to specify all components. Where there is no specification then there is ambiguity and a risk that the final output will not be fit for purpose.

There may be multiple outputs that have to be described.

3.3 Product sequencing

Now that we know what we have to create we can start to think about the sequence that has to happen to achieve a successful conclusion. In PRINCE2 this sequence is shown in the product flow diagram.

Activities and resources will be considered in the next chapter as part of the Developing the Plan stage; however, first we need to develop a greater understanding of the relationships between the outputs and how they depend on each other.

This information will later inform the schedule, the types and numbers of resources and, of course, the costs. A greater level of complexity between the outputs will also increase the level of risk, so it is important to understand the relationships early on.

3.3.1 Technique

An approximate sequence of outputs can often be achieved by turning the product breakdown structure through 90 degrees anticlockwise. The sequence will then run from left to right with the final project products furthest right.

It is important to think in terms of what will be created and to use simple phrases to describe these things. This may seem like unnecessary semantics but it will help to keep focus on what needs to be delivered rather than what needs to be done.

As was shown in the sequence diagram (Figure 3.3), the project cannot proceed on a solid foundation until the performance specification has been defined and sequenced. The sequencing is not visible from the hierarchical product breakdown structure. It is not unusual for the sequencing to cause a rethink in the products that are required or the logical dependencies, and some realignment may be necessary. That is why the Designing the Plan stage is iterative.

3.3.2 Example

Again using the training course example, Figure 3.6 shows the results of turning Figure 3.5 on its side to produce a sequence of outcomes.

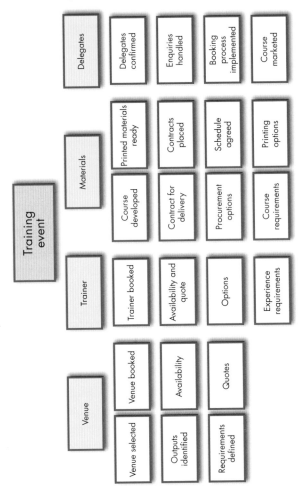

Figure 3.6 A sequence of outputs produced by turning the hierarchical format on its side

3.4 Develop specifications

At this point, we should have a reasonable idea of the main outputs and their subsets, so the process of defining the outputs themselves can begin.

Product specifications are absolutely essential for all projects and are a key element in Developing the Plan.

As well as specifying what we know we also need to think about what we do not know, as otherwise the latter may cause us issues later.

If you are undertaking a project that is creating outputs similar to those in a previous project, then it will make sense to use the other project's product specifications and take advantage of the previous experience.

Tip
The level of granularity at which you provide a description will be variable. As a rule of thumb, if a product feels too big to describe, break it down. However, if you feel that you are stating the blindingly obvious or there is not much to specify then the product may be too small.

3.4.1 Technique

Understanding the technique of creating a product description is essential to documenting specifications. It provides the detail of what is needed to meet the business requirements of the project and, very importantly, the quality criteria against which it will be accepted by the business representative.

It is harder to describe softer products from projects in detail as there may well be a lack of clarity about what has to happen or what will be in place after the change. However, the more detail that can be captured, the less ambiguity there will be, and this will help focus the minds of the project board on the key decisions that will enable clarity and direction.

Detailed product descriptions enable accurate estimating of resources, costs and timescales. The lack of clearly defined product descriptions is a clear indicator that a project is not focusing sufficiently on what it will need to produce.

The product description will also contain the quality criteria for the output, so it is a key contributor to a quality plan for the project.

Table 3.3 lists the headings that should be included in a product description and what should be included in the document.

Tip
At the completion of the Designing the Plan stage, the project should be in a position to seek approval to proceed from the investment decision gate.

Table 3.3 The headings (or fields) to include in a product description

Heading (field)	Content
Reference number	A number that identifies your project, the product and its position in the hierarchy of the product breakdown structure.
Title	The wording to be used to refer to this product.
Purpose	Why the project needs this product and its part in the overall project.
Specification	What the product does, the functionality and interfaces that it will have with other aspects of the project, or the operations that will use it.
Costs	A summary of the cost of the product, including: • Amount of resource effort by type • The costs of the resources • Costs of any assets to be procured • Installation costs • Costs of change, linked to transition activities.
Link to objectives	How this product contributes specifically to the project objectives. The reference numbers of the objectives should be included.
Link to requirements	The contribution that this product will make to satisfy the business requirements. Include any reference numbers.
Form or format	Include if there is a pre-described format for the product. This may point to a template if there is a document or something that is similar in look or feel. Processes and structures are difficult to compare, but projects with harder assets can use this approach.
Derivation	Include details if the product is a subset of another product, or the information used to describe it has been drawn from elsewhere.
Obstacles	Cross-references to specific risks and issues that directly relate to this product and may affect its creation.
Source and skills	A brief summary of the potential sources for this product. Can it be purchased in the marketplace? Or does it have to be created specifically (and if so are those skills available in-house)?
Quality criteria	The tests that will be applied to prove that the product meets the defined specification. The requirements can be regarded as the input specification. The quality criteria are the output specification, which explains what the functionality will be and what levels of performance are acceptable. For a 'soft' project such as a new service, the criteria could be the required performance levels and evidence of trained people in post.
Quality tolerance	This should outline performance or specifications that are beyond the minimum requirements. These may not be required at the point of implementation, and possibly they can be deferred to a later process.
Quality acceptance method	The testing method. This could vary from technical performance tests to a mystery-shopper-type experiential test.
Quality assessment skills	The source of the quality assessor and the skills that they will need to undertake the assessment.

3.4.2 Example

Table 3.4 provides an example of a completed product description for the training course project.

Table 3.4 A product description for the training course project

Heading	Content
Reference number	Ref. no. 001
Title	Delegate confirmed
Purpose	To list the names and contact details, for use by the trainer and the learning and development department for booking arrangements
Specification	The product will hold a list with details for each delegate: • Name • Contact telephone number • Contact email address • Contact line manager's email address
Costs	Travel costs Material costs per head
Link to objectives	Product will contribute to the 'improve the quality of planning across the organization' objective
Link to requirements	All courses to be held in central training facilities (ref. 001)
Form or format	Microsoft Word table printed in A4 portrait mode
Derivation	Potential delegate list: • Email addresses • Telephone book • Organization chart
Obstacles	Contact details may not be up to date
Source and skills	HR staff information Learning and development department competency survey
Quality criteria	Is the list complete? Does the delegate need this function and level of training?
Quality tolerance	Minimum 8; maximum 12 names
Quality acceptance method	Email attachment
Quality assessment skills	Learning and development department manager (approver) Learning and development department Change Governance Support Office (reviewer and coordinator) HR representative (reviewer)

3.5 Role responsibilities for Designing the Plan

The role responsibilities for this stage can be summarized as follows:

- **Project sponsor**
  - Providing leadership and direction in the management of obstacles
  - Valuing good planning and encouraging rigour
  - Intervening to resolve disputes where different parts of the organization have different priorities
  - Approving the business requirements
  - Setting priorities for work
  - Ensuring the right resources are involved in the design of the plan

- **Project manager**
  - Leading the planning activities
  - Ensuring the involvement of people with the right experience
  - Developing the information and documentation to support decision-making
  - Maintaining recorded alignment between the various documents to provide an audit trail of decisions
  - Engaging stakeholders in the process and maintaining communications

- **Business representative**
  - Providing operational knowledge and input to the prioritization of the requirements
  - Helping to prepare product documentation
  - Signing off product descriptions on behalf of the business

- **Suppliers (internal or external)**
  - Providing market knowledge
  - Inputting expert advice to support specifications
  - Advising on ability to achieve within current agreements

- **Project management office/centre of excellence**
  - Advising on other projects that may be generating similar requirements
  - Advising on use of planning framework and techniques
  - Identifying cross-project dependencies and opportunities to remove or exploit
  - Acting as a central repository for project information.

4 Developing the Plan

Now we have gathered the information and analysed the requirements to identify what we have to deliver, we need to develop the plan.

The first key concept within the Developing the Plan stage is to recognize that there may be different levels and views of plans. Appendix 1 provides a summary of plans including those at levels above the project plan. There should be an overarching project plan, and in larger projects this will need to be broken down into a hierarchy of plans (finance, resource etc.) – all with the ability to filter for specific information.

For the majority of projects, there is an overarching project plan and a number of sub-plans (see Figure 4.1). The views (finance plan, resource plan etc.) identified in this diagram will be subsets that run for the life of the project. The quality plan will focus on the assurance and audit aspects of the project.

If the plans are broken down like this, there is a greater degree of granularity and transparency, which will enable the project manager to have greater control. Therefore, early in this stage it is important to decide on the structure of the plans and how these will be built into the overall plan.

Figure 4.1 The project plan and its subsets

The project will have stages that align with the organization's standard project lifecycle if one exists. Each stage should have a specific stage plan, and a number of views may be associated with a particular stage. Figure 4.2 gives an example of how this might work. If the project delivers products into service stage by stage then there may be benefits plans in the scope of the stage plan. There should also be benefit review plans developed for use during the operations phase of the lifecycle after handover.

Another key concept is that of work packages. This is the bundling up of work and its allocation to individuals or groups. In Designing the Plan the concept of outputs was explained. A work package could be the creation of an output or many outputs that are part of the final project. At this point in the development of the plan agreements are made on time and cost and any tolerances for them.

4.1 Stage overview

The starting point for Developing the Plan is the outputs from the previous stage – Designing the Plan. These outputs provide clarity about what needs to be created and delivered, the main sequence of events that we need to plan for, and details of the obstacles (risks and issues) that we are facing.

During the activities at this stage, estimation will be undertaken, effects of the obstacles factored in and then the controls will be designed.

By the end of the Developing the Plan stage the project will be ready for approval and to move into delivery. Figure 4.3 summarizes the inputs, activities and outputs of this stage, and Table 4.1 provides an overview of the tools used.

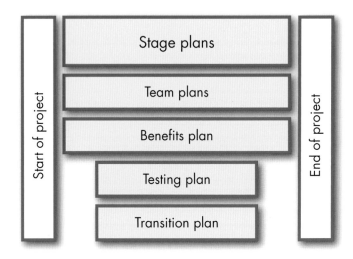

Figure 4.2 Stage plans and associated plans

Figure 4.3 Inputs, activities and outputs of Developing the Plan

Table 4.1 Overview of the tools used in Developing the Plan

Activity	Tool(s)
Develop estimates	Top-down estimating
	Bottom-up estimating
	Parametric estimating (modelling)
	Three-point estimating including Monte Carlo simulation
Review risk	Scenario planning
Set tolerances	Contingency planning
Define the stages	Setting strategic control points
Establish milestones	Milestone identification and analysis
Develop the schedule	Critical path and critical chain analyses
	Gantt chart
Design the controls	Those controls below the stage decision gates, such as the frequency of regular reporting

4.2 Develop estimates

> *A good plan violently executed today is better than a perfect plan next week.*
> George S. Patton Jr

Projects tend to suffer from an optimistic bias, as people tend to have high expectations about the outcome of planned actions. This includes overestimating the likelihood of positive events and underestimating the likelihood of negative events. It is also reflected in overestimation of benefits.

There are a number of reasons for this. These include:

- Lack of experience in the type of change
- Leadership that enforces the ethos of 'just do it'
- Lack of willingness to face up to the reality of how long it will take or how much it will cost
- Capability of the organization to deliver the change
- No basis for estimation, and therefore no basis on which to improve.

When making estimates, it is a common failing to think in terms of how long it will take to get the job done rather than the amount of effort it will take to do the job. These are completely different concepts yet they are often used within projects without this being recognized.

Tip
As part of estimation, we need to understand whether we are talking about 5 days' work, or 1 day's work that will be completed within 5 days. Without this understanding we cannot properly estimate the cost or time required.

To produce effective estimates it is necessary to understand what tasks are required, and what activities need to be undertaken to deliver an output.

As well has having capital costs, each task will take a certain amount of resource effort, and there will be a timeframe within which that resource effort will be undertaken. There are a number of ways of estimating both the effort to do the task and the likely period of time (or duration) needed to complete the task.

There is no substitute for experience when developing estimates. This can be gained from investigating:

- Previous projects
- Other organizations and reference sites that have done this type of project before
- Expertise in the topic area.

All three of these sources are valuable input into the techniques.

There are a number of techniques for estimating, some basic and some more advanced, and these are outlined in the sub-sections below. The project board should be heavily involved in making the decision about which approach to estimating should be used. For example, top-down estimating carries significantly more risk than bottom-up estimating, so the approach selected will reflect the board's appetite for risk and potentially the consequences of failure.

There are areas where the project team may assume that the stakeholder resources will be available and not include them in the estimates, but whether they are available or not could have a big impact on the operational performance. This is why the stakeholders must be involved in the estimation process and sign up to their commitment to the resource levels. Before the project goes forward they must also re-affirm that commitment.

Before estimates are finalized you should agree who is responsible for the following aspects involving stakeholders:

- Meetings to assist with specifications or estimates

- Training

- Workshops for risk or stakeholder analysis

- Testing

- Travelling to the above

- Commenting on documents

- Calls and emails.

4.2.1 Estimating techniques: basic

4.2.1.1 Top-down estimation

Top-down estimation recognizes that there are limitations to what can be achieved and takes the position 'What can we do in x timescale and with y budget?'. The estimate should include things that simply must be done, plus the highest priorities for whatever time/budget is left over.

Back-cast planning

Back-cast planning is useful for 'softer' projects, where the destination is clear but the journey is proving difficult to construct, or there is an immovable deadline imposed externally.

It asks the question 'What will we need to have in place to achieve xxx outcome?' Some people find it easier to work backwards to work out what has to be done. As the technique focuses on the 'must-dos' it can avoid distractions and unachievable requirements and establish the minimum that has to be done and, in effect, the critical path.

Any additional outputs that the project delivers will be negotiable or can be delivered after the non-negotiable deadlines have passed.

Timeboxing

Timeboxing is a technique common in planning projects (typically for software development), where the schedule is divided into a number of separate time periods (timeboxes, normally 2 to 6 weeks long), with each part having its own deadline, deliverables and budget.

Timeboxes are used as a form of risk management, especially for tasks that may easily extend past their deadlines. The end date (deadline) is one of the primary drivers in the planning and should not be changed as it is usually linked to a delivery date for the output. If the team exceeds the deadline, the team has failed in proper planning and/or effective execution of the plan. This can be the result of the wrong people on the wrong job (lack of communication between teams, lack of experience, lack of commitment/drive/motivation, lack of speed) or underestimation of the (complexity of the) requirements.

4.2.1.2 Bottom-up estimation

The bottom-up approach takes a detailed look at the outputs that need to be produced and works out the time and cost to deliver the stated objectives.

Tip
Product-based planning is a bottom-up approach.

Where the estimates exceed the time or cost estimates of the project board, a structured and systematic approach to deciding what must stay in scope and what can be removed needs to be undertaken until the plan meets the aspirations of the board and can be included in the business case. At this point, bottom-up estimating meets top-down estimating.

4.2.1.3 Three-point estimation

Three-point estimation is a popular technique used to estimate the outcome of future events based on very limited information. It should be used for either top-down or bottom-up approaches as a way of establishing a reasonable likelihood of events.

In three-point estimation, three figures (*BC, LC and WC*) are produced initially for every activity that is required to complete the task, based on prior experience or best guesses:

- **Best-case estimate** (BC) Here it is assumed everything goes according to plan, none of the risks materialize and there are no issues.

- **Most-likely-case estimate** (LC) This allows for some risks and issues materializing but assumes that contingency plans work and no major unexpected events happen.

- **Worst-case estimate** (WC) Here everything that could go wrong does, risks materialize, issues are worse than expected and other unexpected events occur. This estimate will reflect the maximum amount of contingency that will be required to deliver the output.

We can then apply a simple formula to achieve the estimate (*E*):

$E = (BC + LC + WC)/3.$

The dividing number can change as your experience increases. This formula works for the first time you do a task, because each option has an equal value. However, if you have done the task 20 times, then your most likely case is based on experience, so you might wish to weight it accordingly to show the increased confidence in the estimate.

4.2.2 Estimating techniques: advanced

There are two more statistically elegant techniques that can be used. These are the programme (or project) evaluation and review technique (PERT) and the Monte Carlo simulation technique.

4.2.2.1 Programme (or project) evaluation and review technique

PERT is a statistical tool used in project management that is designed to analyse and represent the tasks involved in completing a given project. It is commonly used in conjunction with the critical path method where the performance of a task consumes time and requires resources (such as labour, materials, space and machinery). It can be understood as representing the time, effort and resources required to move from one event to another. A PERT activity cannot be performed until the predecessor event has occurred. The estimated duration (TE in the PERT tool) is the best estimate of the time required to accomplish a task, accounting for the fact that things do not always proceed as normal (the implication being that the expected time is the average time the task would require if the task were repeated on a number of occasions over an extended period). The estimate is represented by the formula:

$TE = (O + 4M + P)/6$, where:

O (optimistic time) is the minimum possible time required to accomplish a task, assuming everything proceeds better than is normally expected.

P (pessimistic time) is the maximum possible time required to accomplish a task, assuming everything goes wrong (but excluding major catastrophes).

M (most likely time) is the best estimate of the time required to accomplish a task, assuming everything proceeds as normal.

Be aware that if this is the first time you have done the project or task, the likelihood of best and worst case will be similar. The use of '6' as the division in the formula above assumes that the task has four previous occurrences to draw from. (In previous iterations the likely case has happened four times, but the best and worst case could still occur, so consequently it is divided by 6.)

When the technique is used across a group of activities to achieve a task, it should give a more balanced view of the total time because it will balance the risk of things going well and badly. It is still based on guesstimates if there is no previous experience to draw on, but it reduces the bias described earlier that can affect planning estimates during periods of early optimism!

4.2.2.2 Monte Carlo simulation technique

If we have a critical path network with known dependencies and estimates for optimistic, most likely and pessimistic durations, and we can input any distribution of probabilities, then we can simulate an implementation based on a random assessment of duration for each task. The result is recorded and another simulation is done, and a new recording made. This Monte Carlo simulation calculates the model hundreds or thousands of times, each time using different randomly selected values. When the simulation is complete, we have a large number of results from the model, each based on random input values. These results are used to describe the likelihood, or probability, of reaching various results in the model. We can see the likely durations in a distribution curve showing percentile probabilities of ranges of durations. This method is likely to be used in major engineering projects.

4.2.3 Simple example

A simple example of three-point estimation for someone undertaking a journey is shown in Table 4.2.

Table 4.2 Three-point estimation example

Scenario	Condition	Estimate
Best case	Road is totally clear, all the traffic lights let you straight through and everything works perfectly	2 hours
Most likely case	No breakdowns, but most of the traffic lights are against you and there was heavy traffic in some areas that could reasonably have been expected	4 hours
Worst case	A major accident on one of the roads and a minor breakdown with the car that necessitates a stop-off at a garage	8 hours

Using the formula given above and the figures from Table 4.2, the estimate for the journey would be:

$E = (2 + 4 + 8)/3$

which would give a prudent estimate for the journey of 4 hours and 40 minutes.

4.2.4 Advanced example

For the figures given in Table 4.2, PERT would give:

$TE = (2 + (4 \times 4) + 8)/6 = 4$ hours 20 minutes.

4.3 Review risk

Delays to the project will normally be the result of a risk occurring, and it is therefore prudent to build in contingency or allowance for things going wrong. The calculation of contingency will involve a review of the risk and issue logs, and calculation of the impact of the risk against specific work packages, tasks and activities.

Factors that may increase risk include:

- Dependency on a limited group of resources
- Lack of availability of specific knowledge or skills to deal with the tasks
- Delays in decisions being made
- Lack of availability of funds to pay for the resources
- Confusing the time required to do the task with the period window when it will be done
- Technology or asset performance that was assumed, but was not checked during estimation.

If the resources are in high demand by other projects and there are no alternative suppliers then the risk will increase significantly, in particular the period window when they may be available. It may be 3 hours' work, for example, but if no one is available for 6 months the task will take 6 months.

4.3.1 Technique

This is the point at which you apply your risk and issue management knowledge. The main technique here is scenario planning to check that you have not missed any potential risks. Once you have put your overarching plan together, it is worth standing back and looking at scenarios that could happen, both positive and negative.

Projects rarely fail as a result of one risk or issue. Failure normally results from either:

- A cocktail of threats igniting to cause a major problem, such as when a number of events happen simultaneously, and unforeseen connections cause the totality of the impact to be more severe than the component parts, or
- A sequence of events developing that trigger a risk, followed by knock-on effects that trigger further negative effects, thus causing a much bigger problem than the component parts.

Scenario planning can only really be achieved through a workshop of key people who understand the potential threats and opportunities. It is likely that many of the scenarios that need to be tested have already been identified in the risk and issue logs, but this step is more focused on their cause and the effect on your estimates.

It is important to assess probability, impact and proximity of all risks. Separating the significant few from the trivial helps us to do an aggregation test of 'So what?', which will help to determine the extent to which the risk can be accepted or must be mitigated.

Some scenarios that should be considered with their knock-on effects are listed below:

- Resources available to the project – more or less?

- Costs resulting from procurement – higher or lower?

- Budget – cut or increased?

- Organizational context changes for the project – for example, are there changes of priorities? And are there changes to the organization or project leadership?

- Stakeholder commitment – positive or negative?

The results of considering scenarios will require a review of contingency, and development of alternative approaches and plans. This will involve the development of contingency plans, which will be introduced as 'exception plans'.

A diagram such as Figure 4.4 can be used to map the likelihood and impact of risks. You can also start to draw the potential relationships between risks. For example, in Figure 4.4 Risk A could trigger Risk E and so could Risk B. If Risks A and B are becoming more likely the overall level of risk will be rising. In reality, such a diagram often ends up on an A3 sheet but it is much more effective than long lists of risks.

4.3.2 Example

Table 4.3 lists some scenarios that could cause a shortfall of resources. We have used numbers to illustrate the probability and impact, with 1 being very low and 5 very high. (In this example we ignore proximity but note that it adds a sense of urgency for mitigation.) The multiplication of the probability with the impact gives a number which can then be related to the risk strategy. For example, we may say that scores of 1–6 are low risk, 7–12 are medium risk and 12–25 are high risk.

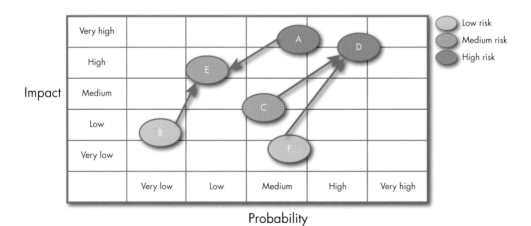

Figure 4.4 Mapping risks against likelihood and impact

Table 4.3 Risk assessment for different scenarios

Scenario/threat	Cause/ event	Probability × impact	Effect	Consequence	Mitigation
Allocated resources become unavailable	Unplanned absence (e.g. sickness)	3 × 2 = 6 (low risk)	Delay	Acceptable delay	Adjust timeline and increase time contingency by 10%
	Planned absence (e.g. holiday)	1 × 1 = 1 (low risk)	Delay	Contingency exists	No effect
Resources costs increase	Resource shortage due to market demand	3 × 4 = 12 (medium risk)	Budget	Increase resource budget	Financial contingency of 20%
Skills not available	Upturn in market demand	4 × 4 = 16 (high risk)	Ability to deliver	Less skilled resources used to deliver the task, which produces lower quality and takes longer to deliver	Reduce acceptance criteria in quality expectation by removing certain acceptance criteria

4.4 Set tolerances

In preparing for battle I have always found that plans are useless, but planning is indispensable. Dwight D. Eisenhower, 1957

The concept of tolerance is used in the context of contingency. Tolerance is the acceptable deviation between what is estimated and what is actually delivered.

There are three major overlapping areas of control in a project (see Figure 4.5):

● The time the project takes

● The resources (cost) used by the project

● The quality of what the project produces.

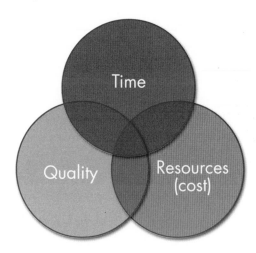

Figure 4.5 Major areas of control in a project

The project must manage all these dimensions as a change to one will affect the others. If the project runs late, it will consume more resources and cost more. The only way to affect this is to change the scope and reduce the quality requirements or amount of what is delivered; this will enable the project to be re-planned, thereby clawing back time and achieving within the same resources (cost). When project managers 'take corrective action' they are trading off these aspects. Clearly they need to know which aspects are the most important.

Tolerance can be allocated against:

- **Budget** The most common tolerance refers to the budget; this allows flexibility on where the money is being spent. For most organizations the budget available to the project manager would only be 90% of the total. This gives some tolerance in the budget and helps to ensure that cost is controlled appropriately and that escalations and changes are managed effectively.

Tip
Tolerance is normally set overall against the budget. This enables the project manager some leeway in balancing the project's costs to keep them within acceptable boundaries, with agreement by the project board.

- **Timescale** By setting a tolerance on the time within which the project or an element of the project can run late, the project may be able to stay within tolerance on quality or cost. It may be that the deadline has no tolerance, and in this case the tolerance will need to be set on quality or budget.

- **Quality** The requirements and product descriptions will set out the acceptable criteria for the quality of the project outputs. It may be that pursuit of perfection will significantly increase the cost of the output, unless it has been set at fixed price. The key to finding tolerance on quality is calculating the time and cost of the minimum functionality; the tolerance can then be set based on the importance of the additional functionality. The timeboxing technique mentioned earlier (see section 4.2.1) can be used to manage the creation of the output.

Having a fixed-price arrangement with external suppliers can reduce the need for contingency on cost, but may result in problems with time and quality if the suppliers' estimates are incorrect. It may cause a management overhead for the project team of encouraging suppliers to deliver. In effect this introduces a secondary risk as the suppliers may underperform.

Remember that projects run a year late one day at a time. Once time slips it cannot be made up without re-planning and/or changes to the way the project is being delivered (taking corrective action). The challenge is to manage the drift of costs, time or quality that aggregates below the radar and becomes transparent late in the day. The tolerance defines whether project managers can deal with slippage themselves, or whether it has to be escalated to the project board.

4.4.1 Technique

Contingency planning is used to manage the risk and set tolerance for the plan. Over and above existing tolerance, there may be a need to develop contingency plans to deal with undesirable scenarios that may develop.

Contingency plans are in effect 'Plan B', to be invoked if 'Plan A' fails or is unachievable.

When establishing tolerance there are two main approaches, and they are linked to the approach that has been taken to estimating.

If the approach to estimating has been top-down, then one of the options is to take a top-down approach to setting tolerance, by having a general tolerance of 10%. If this is done then it should be transparent where the tolerance is going to be used.

If the approach is bottom-up, then the need for tolerance should be less, as the detailed analysis of the dynamics using three-point estimation should even out the estimates and they should be more accurate.

Tip
Critical path analysis, which is explained later (see section 4.7.3), shows the aggregating effect of a delay to a critical activity. Activities on the critical path, by definition, have zero tolerance in terms of time.

Contingency plans should consider and include provision for:

- All the worst-case scenarios developing in the estimations. This enables you to calculate the maximum contingency that would be needed.

- The 'what if' scenarios. These illustrate the knock-on effect if one or a combination of dependent activities suffers a worst-case scenario. This information can be gathered by reviewing risks that have been identified in the risk log but which have not been included in the estimates.

Although not normally considered as part of contingency planning, positive risks or opportunities should be considered as well. Should one or more 'best-case' scenarios develop this may lead to costs from resources and services that are no longer needed or do not have the ability to react to opportunities. Such scenarios could be covered in a Plan C.

4.4.2 Example

Table 4.4 shows a simple contingency plan (Plan A) for setting up a helpline developed using three-point estimates.

Table 4.4 A simple contingency plan for setting up a helpline

Activity	Best case (days)	Likely case (days)	Worst case (days)	Estimate (days)
Performance specified	10	20	80	37
Process A specified	20	25	90	45
Process B specified	20	30	70	40
Information requirements specified	30	45	120	65
Skills specified	5	20	93	39
IT requirements specified	10	25	60	32
Supplier appointed	30	60	150	80
Staff in post	5	30	70	35
Accommodation ready	40	75	205	107
IT ready	20	45	72	46
Service live	**190**	**375**	**1010**	**526**

For simplicity, Table 4.4 assumes all tasks are consecutive and rounds figures in the estimates column. The table shows the best-case scenario is 190 days to deliver the service. With reasonable luck and all things being well it will take 375 days (the likely case scenario), but because of the significant elements of moderation introduced into the three-point analysis by the worst-case scenario (1010 days), the estimate should be 526 days. This estimate therefore allows 150 days' tolerance on the most likely time.

Tip
The sooner the need for contingency is identified and communicated, the less damage will be done to the project's reputation.

In addition to Plan A as developed in Table 4.4, there should also be a Plan B. This should cover:

- What would happen if the aggregating delays erode your tolerance
- What would happen if you are pushed past 526 days
- What you would do about it.

Contingency Plan C should cover:

- How you would cope with aggregating best-case scenarios that may lead to you finishing early
- What you would do about having idle resources (people and money) that would require deployment.

Your options overall for the project include:

- Stopping the project
- Producing a new (exception) plan
- Adjusting the budget (or tolerance)
- Reducing/increasing the quality expectations
- Re-planning against time (giving more time tolerance).

4.5 Define the stages

Management stages are the major board-level control points within the project. Their principal purpose is to stop the project running out of control. Within the organization project lifecycle there are a number of control gates that the project will pass through; these may, or may not, align with the project's technical phases (e.g. software development or construction).

At the end of each management stage, the project should be reviewed for viability before proceeding. This review is normally under the remit of the project board, with advice from the project management office/centre of excellence.

The management stages for an organization specifically relate to the Delivering the Plan stage of the lifecycle, and are specific to the project. Projects of different sizes and risk will need different stages. As a rule, the higher the risk the more frequent the stages.

Project management best practice tends to focus on four generic stages that a project will use, and these apply, to a greater or lesser extent, to the majority of projects. Different methods use different terms, but the Association for Project Management (APM) suggests the following stages:

- Feasibility or concept – can we achieve it?

- Design – create a design

- Develop or build – create or assemble it

- Deploy – transition into service.

4.5.1 Technique

Stages are the strategic control points of the project. At the end of each stage, something tangible should be delivered and a decision should be made on whether to proceed. The end of a stage is likely to link to a significant milestone, achievement or major risk being faced. When defining stages and setting control points it is helpful to consider:

- Focusing resources and activities into a specific type of activity

- Availability of funds and spending them to most effect

- Availability of specific resources

- Maintaining control of direction and stop/go decisions

- Alignment with the proximity of a risk being realized

- Recognizing a point of achievement

- Alignment with a corporate decision or anticipated change

- Alignment with the end of tranche of a programme.

Reviewing the sequencing (see section 3.3) will normally identify major milestones or significant events where stages could be inserted.

4.5.2 Example

In general terms, projects go through a relatively consistent lifecycle. Table 4.5 gives the stages for the helpline example and these should be considered when designing your own plan.

Table 4.5 Lifecycle stages in setting up a helpline service

Stage	Potential scope for the stage
Feasibility	Market analysis
	Consultation with suppliers
	Visits to other organizations that already have a helpline service
	Testing technology to see if it is suitable, or prototyping
	Decision to spend money on design
Design	Design of business models that will be required
	Deciding how the assets/technology will be deployed in detail
	Impact analysis of the change
	Building prototypes for a test area
	Concepts tested and proven
	Decision to spend money and go into development
Develop or build	Building of systems
	Procurement processes
	Contract negotiations
	Human resources change negotiated
	Creation of project outputs
	Acceptance testing
	Piloting
	Planning of transitions
Deploy	Implementation of the systems and processes
	Change-over to new ways of working
	Achievement of the outcomes
	Managing issues

Note that a feasibility project is often separate from the implementation project. By its very nature a feasibility project explores a number of business options and approaches to identify a number of alternative business cases. If, and only if, a single option and approach is identified can we plan for implementation. So, feasibility is often considered as part of an extended lifecycle.

Operations is often shown in the extended lifecycle. It is here that changes may be implemented as post-project tasks – or as separate projects.

4.6 Identify milestones

The word 'milestone' is used extensively but often means different things to different people. Here we use milestone for a task of zero duration that shows an important achievement in a project (it may be an event for celebration).

Milestones are a way of knowing how the project is advancing if you are not familiar with the tasks being executed. They have zero duration because they symbolize an achievement, a point of time in a project.

Tip
Milestones are the dates of the outputs against which your project performance will be monitored, so choose them carefully to ensure they reflect this. Slippage of one milestone will guarantee the others being missed unless there is a change.

Project managers should place several milestones in their schedule at planning time, estimate the milestone completion dates and compare them with the actual completion dates. Milestones should be the minimal points of control in the project for those who are not familiar with it, such as high-level sponsors and executives of the organization.

Best practice in planning a project suggests we place key milestones in the schedule in order to manage stakeholders' expectations. This practice helps your organization define a dashboard for all projects, identify the milestones that have been reached and those that are behind, and manage expectations of those that are involved in the project.

4.6.1 Technique

Your organization's project management office/centre of excellence may define a lifecycle. The milestones are used to monitor the progress of the project and assess whether the estimates were accurate and also to monitor the dependencies of other projects.

Milestones may include:

- The end of a project stage
- A landmark, where there is a visible or tangible achievement
- The completion of a work package (e.g. procurement appoints the contractor/partner); in effect a significant output is delivered
- A point where the project might change its focus (e.g. the building is completed and the focus shifts to moving people in)
- A major decision or dependency that is required but may be outside the project's control – at this point the project must be ready to proceed but will stop if the decision isn't there.

The milestones will normally become evident as the schedule builds, so it is important to baseline your plan before committing to milestones. The outcome relationship model will be a good source for identifying the major milestones for the plan. It is useful to think of milestones in the past tense (e.g. contractor appointed) as this helps to emphasize the achievement of a task or work package.

4.6.2 Example

Table 4.6 gives milestones that could be set during the life of the example helpline project.

Table 4.6 Examples of milestones for the helpline project

Milestone number	Reference
1	Performance specified
2	Process A specified
3	Process B specified
4	Information requirements specified
5	Skills specified
6	IT requirements specified
7	Supplier appointed
8	Staff in post
9	Accommodation ready
10	IT ready
11	Service live

4.7 Develop the schedule

To develop the schedule, it is necessary to know the sequence of events that was defined during the Designing the Plan stage and put a timescale against each one.

There are a number of dependencies that will need to be considered when constructing the schedule:

- The relationships between outputs (also known as dependencies)
- What resources are being used (they can't do two tasks at once)
- Availability of resources, particularly specialists (e.g. legal)
- What assets or services will need to be used to support the tasks (e.g. hardware for prototyping or test lab facilities)
- Governance obstacles, procurement regulations or human resources agreements
- Non-negotiable deadlines (e.g. legal compliance).

Resource planning, critical path analysis (CPA) and Gantt charts are some of the main techniques used while developing the schedule, each of which is described further below.

4.7.1 Technique: resource planning

For the estimation of the resources for the project, products will need to be broken down into tasks and activities, which make up the work packages. Table 4.7 shows how this can be done.

Table 4.7 Tasks, activities and resources associated with a work package

Work package A	Resource A		Resource B		Resource C		Resource D	
Task Y	Time (h)	Period (days)	Time (h)	Period (days)	Time (h)	Period (days)	Time (h)	Period (days)
Activity 1	30	10					4	5
Activity 2			60	20				
Activity 3					10	2		

In Table 4.7, we have a work package A that is made up of a number of tasks. For Task Y, there are three activities. There are four resources involved. Using three-point estimating, we have calculated the time in hours that the task will take and the period in days during which the activity will be undertaken. It is important to recognize these two different variables. The 'period' is the window of time during which the work will be done; there may be many reasons why it extends beyond the actual hours.

Tip
Wherever possible get the person/organization who will do the work to provide the estimates for the times and periods needed for an activity and then gain their explicit commitment to the resourcing profile.

4.7.2 Example: resource planning

The example here (see Table 4.8) is for an office move over the weekend. The estimate has to take account of the following:

- There are 10 people from Operations moving office (hence 10 people each spending 5 hours packing desks in one day)

- There are three facilities management (FM) staff involved in the office move on the Saturday

- One IT person will need to work for a total of 7 hours on the Sunday cabling up the workstations and installing phones

- Health and Safety will need to spend 4 hours checking the workstations and office on the Monday.

Table 4.8 Work package example for an office move

Work package to move office	IT services		FM services		Operations		Health and safety	
Task	Time (h)	Period (days)	Time (h)	Period (days)	Time (h)	Period (days)	Time (h)	Period (days)
Pack up office					50	1		
Relocate desks			24	1				
Cable up workstations	4	0.5						
Install phones	3	0.5						
Carry out safety checks							4	0.5

By adding up the figures entered in Table 4.8 you can see that the total time needed for the move is 85 hours, completed during a period of 3.5 days. What is missing at this stage is the connection and dependency between the tasks and activities, which is picked up later in scheduling.

In calculating the time it is important to focus on the actual hours to get an accurate estimate. The concept of 'person-days' means different things to different people and is open to considerable interpretation so should be avoided.

Once you have worked out the time/resources needed, you can calculate the cost. It is important to keep an audit trail of how you reach your estimates, because should the project be audited or some aspect of the delivery handed over to someone else, they will need to know the basis of your estimation and how you achieved your plan.

The budget for the project can now be established, based on the costs of resources and any external expenditure that is required to purchase assets etc.

4.7.3 Technique: critical path analysis

Using the helpline example we can draw up a product sequence diagram (see Figure 4.6) to illustrate the relationships. It is then possible to use the critical path analysis (CPA) technique to work out how long the project will take and what can or cannot be changed without having an impact on the schedule.

The key information which is required for each task is:

● How long will it take?

● What is the task is dependent on?

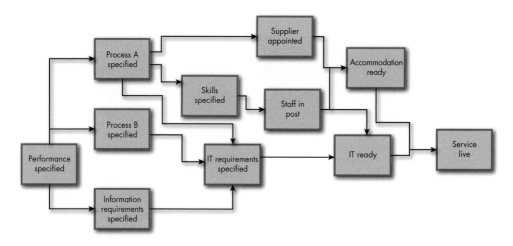

Figure 4.6 A product sequence diagram for the helpline example

4.7.4 Example: critical path analysis

Table 4.9 takes the tasks from Figure 4.6 and adds in information on how long each will take and how it depends on other tasks. For simplicity the periods of time are given in whole days. Using this table it is possible to calculate the earliest point at which the task starts and when it will finish.

From Table 4.9 you can see that the minimum number of days that it will take to deliver the project will be 78 days. It is also possible to deduce which tasks have no flexibility and those that have.

In CPA we simply map the information from Table 4.9 into our product sequence diagram to work out the longest route through the project and identify the tasks that have slack associated with them. Figure 4.7 shows the information contained in each of the task boxes, while Figure 4.8 shows these boxes completed for the helpline example with the critical path shown using a bolder line.

The top row of each of the task boxes identifies the earliest start date (dependent on other tasks) and the task's duration (how long it takes), which then gives you the earliest finish time for the task.

The figures in the bottom row of the task box can be calculated by working backwards from the total length of the project. The latest finish time for each task is the latest start time from the tasks that are dependent on it. The float is the difference between the earliest finish time and the latest finish time. The latest start time is the latest finish time minus the duration.

Table 4.9 Products required and interdependencies

Task	Depends on	Start period	Days	End period
Performance specified	None	0	8	8
Process A specified	Performance specified	8	20	28
Process B specified	Performance specified	8	10	18
Information requirements specified	Performance specified	8	30	38
Skills specified	Process A specified	28	5	33
IT requirements specified	Processes A, B and information requirements specified	38	20	58
Supplier appointed	Process A specified	28	40	68
Staff in post	Skills specified	33	40	73
Accommodation ready	Supplier appointed, staff in post	73	5	78
IT ready	IT requirements specified	58	10	68
Service live	IT ready, accommodation ready	78	0	78

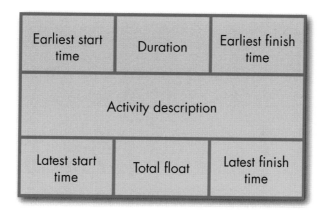

Figure 4.7 Information to fill in for each task box in critical path analysis

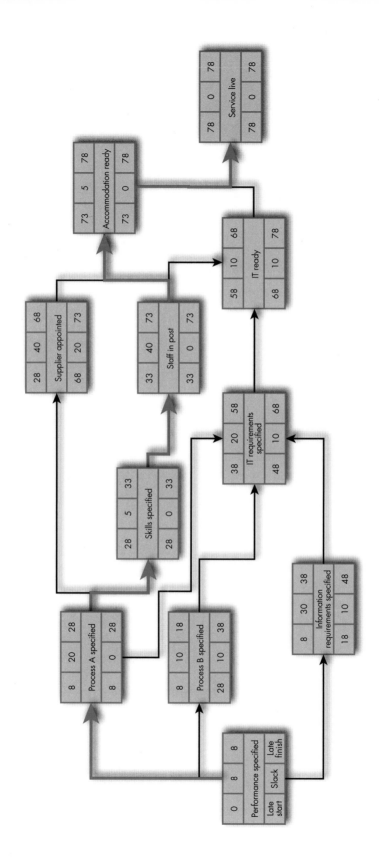

Figure 4.8 Data mapped into the product sequence diagram and the resultant critical path

The tasks with zero float represent the critical path for the project and should be managed intensively. The tasks that have some float have slack that can be used to make sure that time isn't lost on the critical path.

Behind each one of these tasks there will be a three-point estimate that has led you to the calculation of the effort required. If any of the resources are deployed on parallel tasks you need to be aware of it, as this means the tasks must become consecutive or will need float to enable them to happen in the timescale.

The critical path tasks could be used for the project milestones.

4.7.5 Technique: Gantt chart

The information required for the scheduling is usually stored in varying levels of detail in tables and diagrams but these may not be easy for people to follow. It is therefore good practice to also have a simple graphical illustration (a Gantt chart) of the project to show the tasks against a time line. A Gantt chart can easily be created using spreadsheet, diagramming or project management software.

4.7.6 Example: Gantt chart

Figure 4.9 is the same project that was used in Figure 4.8 but illustrated against a timeline of days and created in a spreadsheet.

4.7.7 Finalizing the resource plan

Once the schedule is in place it is possible to finalize the resource plan. Each area that provides resources, internal or external, should be consulted and asked to commit to providing the specified resources when they are needed. A common fault in project planning is to assume that internal groups, in particular, can produce resources when they are needed and without warning.

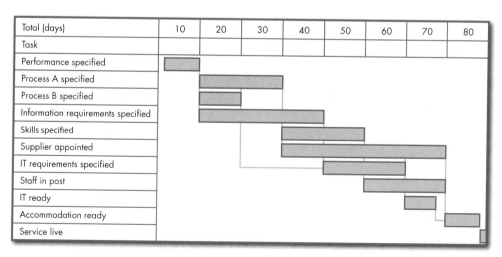

Figure 4.9 Gantt chart example

4.8 Design the controls

If there are not appropriate controls in place the project will lose momentum and focus and stray off course. The problems may take time to become evident, but it is worth remembering that projects do not go wrong overnight. They go wrong because of small and unnoticed changes or failures that in themselves don't alert the project board, but when aggregated can lead to failure and waste.

To establish good controls the project must have the following fundamentals in place before moving into delivery:

- A project board with the competencies to manage a project of this size
- Clear responsibilities for all members of the team and roles assigned specifically for controls
- A baseline project plan within which there are solid estimates
- Internal and external suppliers who have explicitly signed up to their commitments within the project plan or the resource plan
- A budget, and agreement that funds will be made available to meet the expenditure plan
- A process for handling change requests, however small
- Stage plans, where appropriate
- Set tolerances
- A set of work packages that will deliver the outputs
- Arrangements to undertake assurance reviews of project management effectiveness
- Assurance reviews on the quality of the work on schedule to meet the quality requirements of product descriptions.

Tip
At this point the project should be ready for a decision gate as part of the project lifecycle.

In a larger, more formal project it would be appropriate to have a formal quality plan that outlines how this control will work.

When designing the controls, it is important to include formal estimation of what resources will be required to:

- Undertake the reviews
- Participate in the reviews
- Deal with the actions resulting from the reviews.

4.8.1 Technique

The main control technique is the process design for the main control areas or themes. In simple terms, this is the design for how you will manage and control the themes that will help you to be successful. The following are the main themes for which there should be a defined approach and scope within which project team members can operate before needing to escalate an issue:

- Quality

- Risk

- Issue

- Budget

- Information and configuration management

- Resource and team management

- Stakeholder and communications

- Project governance and reporting

4.8.2 Example

Table 4.10 is an example listing the key components needed for effective risk management, but the same or very similar factors will apply to each of the control areas listed above.

Figure 4.10 is an illustrative diagram showing a process model for identifying risks. Especially in a large project, this kind of diagram will help everyone to understand what is going on and who is responsible for what.

4.9 Role responsibilities for Developing the Plan

The role responsibilities for this stage can be summarized as follows:

- **Project sponsor**
  - Providing leadership and direction in the management of obstacles
  - Valuing good planning and encouraging rigour
  - Resolving disputes where different parts of the organization have different priorities
  - Approving the estimates
  - Setting priorities for milestones
  - Ensuring the right resources are involved in the design of the plan
  - Ensuring the levels of controls for delivery are appropriate

Table 4.10 Factors to consider in designing controls for risk management

Roles, accountabilities, responsibilities and activities	**Project sponsor** Encouraging an open approach to risk recognition Monitoring and review of project risks Identification and ownership of external risks Supporting the project manager in delivering mitigation plans Ensuring compliance with the organization's best practice **Project manager** Managing the risk processes Identifying and capturing risks Maintaining risk information Reporting on risk exposure Escalating to project sponsor in line with approach Undertaking risk impact assessments
Processes, tools and techniques to be used	Organization/centre of excellence risk management process
Standards to be applied (in-house or regulatory)	Organization/centre of excellence risk management process
Escalation routes and triggers for interventions	Risks that could potentially cause the project to exceed tolerance Risks that threaten dependencies on other projects
Subject matter experts to be consulted	Organization risk manager
Allocated budget to cover activities	Included within project management costs
Criteria for measuring success and assurance/ review arrangements	Review will be at gate review Numbers of recorded issues that should have been identified as risks Numbers of risks becoming issues
Definition of key terms	Organization/centre of excellence risk management process
Activities to implement the approach	Undertake risk workshop Capture and analyse risks Establish and baseline risk register Establish monthly reporting to project sponsor Establish monthly reporting to project management office/centre of excellence

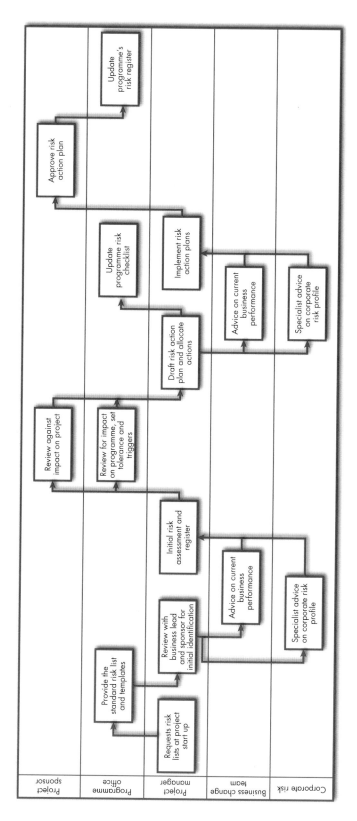

Figure 4.10 Risk identification and analysis

- **Project manager**
  - Leading the planning activities
  - Ensuring people with the right expertise are involved in the estimation process
  - Developing the information and documentation to support decision-making
  - Designing the stages
  - Designing the controls
  - Developing the milestone plan and the schedule
  - Engaging stakeholders in the process and maintaining communications

- **Business representative**
  - Providing operational knowledge and input to the prioritization of the requirements
  - Helping to prepare product documentation
  - Signing off resource commitments on behalf of the business

- **Suppliers (internal or external)**
  - Providing market knowledge
  - Inputting expert advice to support specifications
  - Advising on ability to achieve within current agreements
  - Signing off resource commitments on behalf of their organization

- **Project management office/centre of excellence**
  - Advising on other projects that may be generating similar requirements
  - Advising on use of planning framework and techniques
  - Identifying cross-project dependencies and opportunities to remove or exploit, in order to gain efficiencies
  - Acting as a central repository for project information
  - Approving project controls.

5 Delivering the Plan

The key to effective project control is to measure actual progress and compare it with planned progress on a timely and regular basis, taking any necessary corrective action immediately.

During delivery of the plan, the controls will need to be continuous. Deviations can occur for any number of reasons and manifest themselves in different ways. Most projects will go wrong one day at a time, and the key is recognizing the aggregating effect of deviations as much as trying to avoid major problems. Table 5.1 provides an overview of the tools that are used in this stage.

Table 5.1 Overview of the tools used in Delivering the Plan

Activity	Tools
Establish controls	Change control
Manage stakeholders	Stakeholder perception tracking
Manage time	Gap analysis against schedule
Manage cost	Gap analysis against budget
Manage quality	Quality review and exception reporting
Capture lessons learned	Identifying and capturing

Tip
Having a wonderful plan without good controls is a bit like preparing a fabulous meal and not bothering to set the oven timer to ensure it is properly cooked. In this chapter we use survival tips to help focus on controlling the plan.

5.1 Stage overview

This stage covers the management of the plan as the project moves into delivery. The plan should already have specified all the elements and controls so we now move into the management of control and reacting to change.

Figure 5.1 summarizes the inputs, activities and outputs of this stage.

Figure 5.1 Inputs, activities and outputs of Delivering the Plan

As with each stage, the inputs will already have been created and developed in earlier stages. Once Delivering the Plan is completed, the planning project will be ready to close.

The steps focus on the four areas of stakeholders, time, cost and quality that, if not managed properly, will be the sources of failure, or perceived failure. The final step relates to lessons learned, which is essential if the quality of planning is to improve for individuals, teams and the organization.

There is a basic cycle (Figure 5.2) that will now be managed through to the end of the project:

● Implementation of the plan and establishing the controls

● Monitoring the progress of the project against the baseline in the plan, with particular reference to effectiveness of the estimates and the performance of resources against those plans

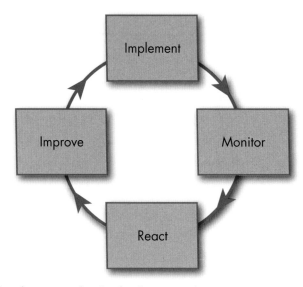

Figure 5.2 Cycle of activities for the final stages of a project

- Reacting to changes or evidence that the project will not stay within its tolerance levels and re-planning accordingly

- Identifying opportunities to improve and implementing them.

This cycle applies for each of the four control areas, namely time, cost, quality and stakeholders.

5.2 Establish controls

Depending on what controls you have planned to put into place, establishing them will require focus. At the start of the project there will be energy to move into delivery and start to create things and as a consequence there will be plenty of parallel activity, which will need to be controlled.

The focus of the project manager must be to establish control of what is going on. They should avoid the temptation to let things roll and worry about reporting in a month or so. Control is a daily activity not a monthly report. It is recommended that project managers spend at least 10–20% of their time doing management tasks such as logging and tracking issues and risks and recording progress against plan. The key principles of control will be based on:

- **Control of change** This is essential, as changes of any sort will have an impact on one or more of time, cost, quality or stakeholder perception. Therefore change must be carefully controlled. There must be a formal process in place with an impact assessment for each change request, and these should be approved by the project board. Small, uncontrolled changes are a major risk to the project achieving its objectives.

- **Timely and accurate information** Information should be relevant to the controls in question and relate to the four areas of control. Lack of or poor-quality information about project performance is evidence of lack of control. The information that is collected should be directly valuable to the control process. It is common for projects to provide prescriptive updates on progress explaining what they have achieved. However, you should report statistics against the baseline wherever possible, and focus on the facts.

- **Evidence-based progress** This means being able to see tangible proof of progress before accepting it has happened. Such proof can range from receiving a draft report to seeing the foundations of a building.

- **Monitoring as you go** If you monitor as you go this will save time and pain later trying to collect the evidence. Owners of work packages should report to the project on a regular basis; if they are on the critical path it should be weekly at a minimum. The focus is on identifying early-warning indicators from the work packages: extinguishing small fires now is easier than fighting large fires later!

● **Involvement of the team** Involving the team in the process of control is essential. There is a natural resistance to control and reporting, particularly if people don't understand the relevance, so gaining the team's commitment is essential. When the team understands the bigger picture of the project, they may well identify issues in their work packages that may be of little interest to them but may be a major threat or opportunity to other parts of the project.

Tip
Team dynamics and performance are a key area to focus on. If a team works and communicates well, the controls will work more effectively.

5.2.1 Technique

The principal technique in this activity is change control. There are a number of steps that all changes should follow to ensure that their impact on the project is understood.

Change control is normally linked to issue management. Changes will tend to result from an issue being raised by someone, so the start of the change process is the issue log.

As with many things in project management, it is small uncontrolled changes that can aggregate to create major problems later, so the earlier control is established the better. The change control process should be defined when the controls are designed.

The basic steps of change control are listed in Table 5.2.

After an issue has been logged, the next step is to draw up a change request relating to it, wherever possible using standard headings (see Table 5.3). This will make it easier to assess the impacts of the change and record decisions made about it.

Table 5.2 Steps for change control

Step	Description
Identify the change	Log the requirement in the issue log and describe what is actually required in a change request. Having a way of categorizing the issue will help; for example, categorizing the issue as business process, technical or HR will give you a good starting point.
Prioritize	Give the change a priority. Is it urgent in so far as it needs to be done quickly to avoid further problems, or is it something that can wait?
Assess the impact	This step should thoroughly review the effect this change will have on the project. This impact assessment should be undertaken against the four control areas of time, cost, quality and stakeholders. In addition, if benefits are a key justification for the project, then benefits analysis should also be undertaken.

Table continues

Table 5.2 *continued*

Step	Description
Analyse the options	There may be a number of ways of meeting the new requirement or dealing with the problem. Each should be analysed against the following criteria: • Likelihood of success • Timescale • Dependency with and impact on other outputs • Impact on business case (cost and benefits) • Impact of doing nothing • Impact on external dependencies • Impact on tolerance.
Authorize variation	As part of the control design, levels of delegated authority should have been set. These will dictate what can be authorized by the project manager and what will need to go to the project board, or even the programme board, for approval. If the change is rejected, it is very important that the reasons for rejection are recorded and communicated to the stakeholder in the change. This will help people understand why something that seemed like a good idea was not approved. It also provides an audit trail of the decision, so that if the issue arises again the previous analysis will still be available. Assurance/audit reviews may also focus on this area.
Build and test the solution	If approval is given then the change would become a work package with the normal controls. The change solution would need to undergo feasibility, development and testing to ensure it meets the performance and budget expectations and that it interfaces with other outputs effectively.
Implement and monitor	Implementation will need to be planned. It may be included within a current stage or scheduled for roll out in a later stage. Changes will need to be packaged together in the most appropriate way to minimise disruption and maximize value for money. Monitoring the impact on live operations and existing processes and service levels could be part of the process, to ensure that capability achieved in previous stages has not become de-stabilized.
Review and update the documentation	Once the change is implemented, any product descriptions or benefits profiles that have been affected should be updated, along with any revisions to the plans. The issue log and change request should also be updated.
Capture lessons learned	If the change is significant, then holding a post-implementation review to reflect on what went well and what didn't, and to capture these in the project lessons learned report, will help ensure that future changes are handled optimally.

5.2.2 Example

In order to control changes and their impacts it is important that each change requested is documented. Table 5.3 is an example of a request for a change from specifying desktop to specifying laptop computers within a project's plan.

Table 5.3 Example of a change request

Change title	Change from desktop to laptop machines
Change description	It is proposed that the standard hardware used for IT desktops be changed to laptops to enable greater flexibility within the office area and provide the opportunity to include home working. This will enable expansion of the staff numbers by flexible working without the need to increase office space.
Priority	Urgent. The orders for the IT hardware will need to be raised in the next 3 weeks.
Impact	The change will increase the costs but will offer benefits. There are no other impacts on the project.
Options	Do nothing and stick with the current plan. Make the change and create the opportunity for efficiencies once the service is live.
Benefits	Better use of office space in the future. Potential for home working.
Costs	Estimated increase on desktop hardware budget is 30%.
Decision	Required within 2 weeks.

5.3 Manage stakeholders

Reviews by the UK National Audit Office have shown that stakeholder perception of a project is often totally unrelated to the traditional performance measures of time, cost and quality. The key to successful management of stakeholders is setting realistic expectations and then maintaining engagement through regular communications that reinforce expectations at the appropriate level.

There is a tendency to communicate with stakeholders at the start of the project when the requirements are being identified, lose contact during planning and delivery, and re-engage near to transition time. However, and disappointingly for the project, by this time the stakeholders may have lost interest. Therefore, ideally, stakeholders should be involved during the design and development of the plan, but even if this hasn't happened, they certainly need to be engaged during the delivery of the plan.

As we noted above, a key aspect of stakeholder management is expectation setting. One of the problems with delivering any sort of change is that it may be good for the organization but it is quite often bad for individuals. It is therefore essential that the project communicates effectively and ensures that there is a realism about the impact on operations and individuals when the project delivers. This is particularly important when planning for transition.

Transition is often painful for the operational people who have to deal with the new ways of working, especially if they are not adequately supported during this period. As the resistance to the change increases, the chances of success are reduced and the image of the project is tarnished, however well it is delivered.

Tip
A study at the Vehicle and Operator Services Agency (VOSA) in 2007 showed that for every project person accounted for in business cases, three operational people were being used and were unaccounted for. This illustrates why it is essential to fully understand the impact of changes and how resources are being consumed and accounted for.

A particular issue about which the project must be sensitive is the amount of resources that are expected from stakeholders. Stakeholders may resist a project because of the resources they are expected to provide rather than simply being against the concept of the project.

With huge pressure being placed on front-line services there will often be little flexibility in the resources that they can take from delivering services to support the project. As part of estimating you may have provided backfill, but having more bodies can often reduce efficiency. It is also likely that the project will want access to the best operational people to support the change, but these are exactly the people the operations will not want to lose.

5.3.1 Technique

At the outset of the project during the Defining the Plan stage (see section 2.2 and Table 2.3), stakeholder analysis should have been undertaken to underpin communications planning. This early analysis should show where the levels of support and engagement are. However, during the following stages of the plan more information and understanding will have been developed and stakeholder perceptions may have changed. These changes of perception will need to be tracked, as the aggregating support or resistance from stakeholders will increase or decrease the risk to the project.

You can gather intelligence on stakeholder perceptions by:

● Monitoring responses and feedback to communications – positive, negative or none

● Noting views expressed at meetings or in one-to-one conversations

● Noting views expressed through other media

● Recording attendance/availability for meetings

● Conducting surveys

● Hosting consultation workshops/events.

5.3.2 Example

Stakeholder support should be captured regularly and be part of the project reporting process, as movements in support may well be an early indicator of problems ahead.

During delivery, the analysis is even more important, and the project should be looking to leverage opportunities to win support from stakeholders who are resistant. This can be achieved through using quick wins or carefully targeting stakeholders to be involved in the pilots or testing to help them increase their involvement.

Table 5.4 is a simple table (similar to Table 2.3) which maps stakeholders' support against the project objectives for a certain month (say April) of a project. At this time Objective 1 has full support but the support is not quite so good for other aspects of the project, which may be more or less critical.

Table 5.5 shows the support 3 months later (July in this example). The level of support for Objective 1 has weakened, support for Objective 3 has strengthened and Stakeholder 1 is looking very unhappy. This information would now feed into the communications plan for the next 3 months. Priorities might include communications with Stakeholder 1 to try to reduce their opposition and attempts to communicate more clearly about certain objectives (e.g. Objective 1).

Table 5.4 Stakeholder support mapped to project objectives (April)

April	Objective 1	Objective 2	Objective 3	Objective 4	Objective 5
Stakeholder 1	1	3	2	1	2
Stakeholder 2	1	3	2	3	2
Stakeholder 3	1	3	2	3	1
Stakeholder 4	1	1	3	1	1
Stakeholder 5	1	1	3	1	1

Key ■ (3) = resistor; ■ (2) = ambivalent; ▨ (1) = supporter.

Table 5.5 Stakeholder support mapped to project objectives (July)

July	Objective 1	Objective 2	Objective 3	Objective 4	Objective 5
Stakeholder 1	3	3	2	1	2
Stakeholder 2	1	2	1	3	2
Stakeholder 3	1	2	1	3	1
Stakeholder 4	2	1	3	1	1
Stakeholder 5	3	2	3	1	1

Key: as for Table 5.4.

5.3.2.1 Support change analysis

Adding numbers to the status map allows for a comparison of stakeholder to be drawn between the two months (Table 5.6). This can also be displayed in a graph to show whether support has changed for each objective or whether one stakeholder has changed opinion for a number of objectives (Figure 5.3).

Table 5.6 Change in stakeholder support from April to July

	Objective 1	Objective 2	Objective 3	Objective 4	Objective 5
Stakeholder 1	–2	0	0	0	0
Stakeholder 2	0	1	1	0	0
Stakeholder 3	0	1	1	0	0
Stakeholder 4	–1	0	0	0	0
Stakeholder 5	–2	–1	0	0	0

5.4 Manage time

The baseline schedule for the plan is the measure of success for the project. If the project starts one day late, it will finish one day late. Time that has passed has gone forever, so there is no flexibility on time as such. However, once the critical path is in place, it is possible to identify the activities that have some flexibility and the resources can be managed around this.

Managing time starts with establishing a baseline plan that shows how the project scope will be accomplished on time and within the budget. Once this baseline plan is agreed

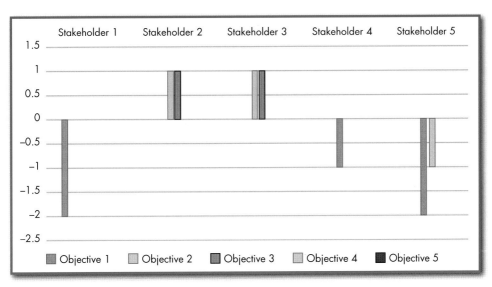

Figure 5.3 Graph of change in stakeholder support from April to July

with the business representative, the project starts. A regular reporting period should be established for comparing the actual progress with the planned progress. Reporting may be daily, weekly or monthly, depending on the complexity and duration of the project. During each reporting period, two kinds of data or information need to be collected:

- Data on actual performance

- Information on any changes to the project scope, schedule or budget.

Once the updated schedule and budget have been produced, they need to be compared with the baseline schedule and budget and analysed for variances to determine whether the project is ahead of or behind the time schedule. The project control process continues throughout the project.

If the planned corrective actions do not result in an acceptable schedule, these steps will need to be repeated. Throughout a project, each time the schedule is recalculated it is necessary to analyse the newly calculated schedule to determine whether it needs further attention. If the project begins to run late, then it is essential that the project board is advised of the likely impact at the earliest opportunity. If the project has had tolerance set centrally (e.g. by a project management office or centre of excellence), then the impact assessment will take into account whether the delay will threaten the ability to remain inside that tolerance.

Projects usually run late as a result of a combination of minor delays rather than a single major delay. The key to maintaining a realistic and achievable schedule is to learn from the delays and understand why the estimates were incorrect.

5.4.1 Technique

Time management analysis should be based on the expected delivery timescale and the consumption of any tolerance that may been allocated to the project. It involves the following four steps:

- Analysing the schedule against the baseline, identifying any gaps and determining which areas may need corrective action

- Deciding what specific corrective actions should be taken

- Revising the plan to incorporate the chosen corrective actions

- Recalculating the schedule to evaluate the effects of the planned corrective actions.

Delays should be assessed by considering their impacts on the following:

- Milestones

- Resource plans

- Dependent outputs

- Programme plan if appropriate

- Finance plan
- Transition plans
- Operational business plans
- Benefits plans.

5.4.2 Example

Once a milestone has been missed it is guaranteed that the remainder will be missed as well, so a total recasting of the plan is required to establish a credible revised plan. The critical path analysis (CPA) should give the impact assessment for the change. A variation report like that shown in Table 5.7 could be used to illustrate the impact assessment.

Table 5.7 lists the 'likely case' times from Table 4.4 as the planned days, and the three-point estimates from the same table as the planned days in tolerance. As can be seen, some of the estimates were way out, some slightly bad, some slightly good and some quite accurate. It is useful to produce such a table to illustrate and raise awareness of activities that are running late; however, in this example the total aggregated days generally stayed within the three-point estimated tolerance, so although the project delivered late it remained under control but on the edge of tolerance all the way through.

Table 5.7 Variation report for planned versus actual time

Activity	Planned days	Planned days in tolerance	Actual days	Aggregating days using tolerance	Total aggregated days
Performance specified	20	37	35	37	35
Process A specified	25	45	30	82	65
Process B specified	30	40	90	122	155
Information requirements specified	45	65	25	187	180
Skills specified	20	39	25	226	205
IT requirements specified	25	32	50	258	255
Supplier appointed	60	80	45	338	300
Staff in post	30	35	90	373	390
Accommodation ready	75	107	80	480	470
IT ready	45	46	44	526	514
Service live	**375**	**526**	**514**	**526**	**514**

5.5 Manage cost

Performance against forecasted budget is an essential reporting requirement. The main costs for a project will come under two headings: resources and assets. The control activities around costs are very much linked to the controls around time as the time required from the resources represents significant costs.

The costs of assets should be known or established as part of the procurement process, either through formal tendering or gaining quotations. Variations in cost are likely to be linked to changes in requirements or specification by the operational areas or the suppliers offering additional facilities that increase the costs. Any changes to cost must be raised as a change request and managed through change control.

If the project business case is justified on benefits, careful monitoring of the changes from the baseline cost estimate against the planned benefits is essential. There may be a tipping point where the benefits are no longer achievable and the project should be stopped, and the earlier this is spotted the better.

Earlier in the project, estimates will have been created for the different types of resource. Although not all of these are tracked as costs because they are internal, availability, performance and consumption of these resources will all be critical success factors for the project, for the following reasons:

● Using external resources at a faster rate than was anticipated will cause problems with later tasks

● Using operational resources earlier than planned will mean they may not be available later

● Over-utilization of operational resources that have not been accounted for may alienate the stakeholders and lead to loss of cooperation

● Being under budget against the plan could mean that the project is either ahead of or behind schedule. This could be because the expenditure is being postponed due to procurement delays.

It is important to assess, as early as possible, whether resources are being over-utilized or are not available when required. This information should be used to re-assess the plan and, if necessary, to recast the stage plan at least. Some reasons for resource estimates being wrong include:

● Estimates being based on wrong comparisons or experiences

● Individual or group competencies being inadequate

● Over-reliance being placed on one or two key individuals

● Underestimating the complexity of the tasks that contribute to asset costs

- Stakeholders failing to deliver their commitments or delaying procurement

- Resource conflicts with other projects operating in that area, and operations being overcommitted

- Events in the supply chain or operations drawing on resources that were anticipated as being available to projects

- Assets not actually being available for procurement

- Assets not meeting specification.

5.5.1 Technique

As with time management, the cost analysis should be based on the expected costs and the tolerance that may have been allocated to the project. The technique for managing costs is also essentially the same as for managing time, namely:

- Analysing the budget against the baseline and determining which areas may need corrective action

- Deciding what specific corrective actions should be taken

- Revising the plan to incorporate the chosen corrective actions

- Recalculating the budget to evaluate the effects of the planned corrective actions.

Delays should be assessed by considering their impacts on the following:

- Capital budget

- Revenue budget

- Expenditure profile

- Projected availability of funds

- Benefits plan.

5.5.2 Example

Table 5.8 shows variation between planned and actual costs using the same example as in the previous section.

In the example in Table 5.8, the project comes in over budget because of a significant later overspend on IT and accommodation, but is still within overall tolerance.

Table 5.8 Variation report for planned versus actual cost

Activity	Baseline cost estimate	Costs including tolerance	Actual cost	Aggregating baseline including tolerance	Total actual cost compared to tolerance
Performance specified	20	15	15	15	15
Process A specified	10	45	12	60	27
Process B specified	10	40	12	100	39
Information requirements specified	5	20	10	120	49
Skills specified	5	7	4	127	53
IT requirements	20	32	50	159	103
Supplier appointed	12	20	17	179	120
Staff in post	30	40	39	219	159
Accommodation ready	100	120	130	339	289
IT ready	100	120	140	459	429
Service live	**312**	**459**	**429**	**459**	**429**

5.6 Manage quality

We haven't got time to do it right, but we have got time to do it again (... and again). Claire Rookes

Managing quality is about getting the outputs right first time. What the project doesn't want to happen is something completely different from what was required turning up on site on the day of installation.

The other aspect to quality is the evolving expectations of stakeholders. They may have specified one thing, but in their mind's eye it has morphed into something completely different through overpublicizing the benefits or the positives. This might lead to a perceived project failure.

Quality is managed by measuring and monitoring the quality of the outputs being developed against the quality criteria defined during design and development rather than waiting to see the finished article, when much time and effort may have been wasted creating the wrong thing.

The sources of acceptable criteria were defined in the product descriptions and these should provide the basis for the assessment process. Keeping the delivery of the output on track may be achieved by establishing reviews at key points where deviations can be managed, namely:

- Agreeing the outline design
- Building the prototype to prove the concept
- Functional testing to prove it does what it says
- Piloting to test it in a live environment
- Final roll-out.

Each of these review points may trigger payments, which is a good way to control the expenditure related to value delivered. These steps could also be used to measure the percentage of the task completed.

Reviews can take two forms: a formal scheduled review and/or spot checks on progress.

Opportunities may arise through the quality control process to deliver requirements that were identified at the outset, but were left out of scope as they were categorized as 'nice to haves', thus increasing value to the operations. Alternatively, a completely new opportunity may arise unexpectedly.

Changes to quality should be regarded as issues and follow the change control procedures. Any changes to requirements from either the supplier or the business representative will have a time and cost impact which must be assessed.

5.6.1 Technique

The main technique for assuring quality is the quality review. This is a structured approach to checking that progress is being made and is on track for the delivery of an output. It can be used to check any of the outputs, whether they are hard or soft, but may require some flexibility in assessing progress.

Product descriptions include the functionality and performance required of the output and the quality criteria against which acceptance will be made. These are key to assessing quality. In particular, look at the essential functionality to meet the acceptance criteria and those areas of functionality which are nice to have but not essential.

The technique for the review should follow the steps described in Table 5.9.

Table 5.9 Review techniques for quality assurance

Step	Description
Plan the review	Scope the review and identify what will be reviewed.
	Review the product description and decide how the review will be undertaken.
	Identify the evidence that will be required to illustrate progress.
	Identify the resources that will be required – in particular if there are any specialists or subject matter experts who will need to support the project team.
	Communicate the plan to the owners of the product and schedule the review.
Undertake the review	Inspect the product description to establish what evidence should be in place.
	Inspect the output as it stands for evidence of tangible progress (i.e. what actually exists at the moment, not what you are being told exists). Evidence could include reports, designs, visible construction, ICT being installed etc.
	Conduct interviews with key individuals to gather their opinions and views on progress towards the delivery of the outputs.
	Note that where evidence is not available, the output will have failed the review. Where there is evidence, but it does not meet the specification of the product descriptions, then again it will have failed the review. Remember, there is no such thing as 'nearly done'; only evidence can be used to measure progress, not oral or written promises.
Report results	If the inspections show that the output is on schedule and meeting the quality criteria, no action should be taken.
	If the output is either exceeding or failing to meet expectations an off-specification report should be generated to the project board. This should outline where the issues are and include an impact assessment on the project and dependencies. The project board will then decide whether action is required or whether to accept the deviation as part of its tolerance and contingency.
Exception plan	If there is a decision to take action on addressing the quality failures and the impact on the project, the project board would instruct the project manager to develop an exception plan to ensure that the project will meet the required quality standards.
	This plan should use the steps defined within change control to identify, assess impact and offer an options analysis for the project board to base its decision on.
Close	The actions defined in the exception plan should now be embedded in the project plan.

5.6.2 Example

Table 5.10 is an example of what a report from a quality review might include.

Table 5.10 Example of what to include in a quality report

Headings	Content
Product description	This should be drawn from the project document and summarize what is being investigated.
Acceptance criteria	Outline what was expected and the source of this expectation. This may be functional specifications or other information included within the product description.
Management overview	An overview of the process that was followed and the results. This information will be key to communicating with stakeholders, including the project board.
Review team	Describe who was involved and why. It is essential that the review has independence from the process of creating the output. This can be achieved by using project resources or expertise from outside the project.
Level of confidence	A simple three-level rating that reflects the overall confidence of the review team that the output will be fit for purpose. It should be based on the evidence that has been produced and the confidence that the output will meet its deadline and functionality based on the objective assessment.
Results of tests	Detailed report showing the tests that were carried out and the conclusions from the results. This should specifically focus on compliance with existing quality criteria.
Issues that have arisen	Issues that have been identified that should now be noted in the project issue log relating to current or projected failure of the output to meet specification, or threats and opportunities of these variations.
Recommended action	Recommended actions from the review on how the issues can be resolved.

5.7 Capture lessons learned

We learn from history that we do not learn from history.
Georg Wilhelm Friedrich Hegel

It is highly unlikely that the estimates for the project or stages will be correct first time, unless it is a project where there is a lot of experience and track record to draw on. So expect the plan to be recast and lessons to be learned; this is not failure, it is part of gaining experience and improving.

Tip
Acknowledging lessons to be learned is not acknowledging failure; failure to acknowledge and learn from lessons is the true failure.

Some lessons will be a reaction to unexpected events, while others will emerge simply from experience.

Lessons learned should be captured and shared with the project board openly and the impact of the lessons on this project and other projects should be understood.

5.7.1 Technique

One of the problems that organizations suffer from when managing lessons learned is that this activity is often left until the end of the project, when the lessons have been forgotten about or it is too late to benefit from them.

Lessons should be learned from day 1 of the project and continue to be learned until the project closes, so it should be a continuous activity to learn and improve. A good project manager will collect lessons learned as they happen, and, as a minimum, lessons should be learned and captured at the end of a stage. Lessons learned can be captured in a number of ways:

- Identifying them and including them in monthly progress reports
- Hosting workshops at key points in the project lifecycle to gather views on what has been learned and report to the project management office/centre of excellence accordingly.

Areas where valuable lessons for others might arise include:

- Accuracy of estimates
- Resource productivity
- Effectiveness of the project board
- Reliability of suppliers, in-house and external
- Risk and issue identification and impact assessments
- Unforeseen events that should have been predicted
- Project management support
- Realism and engagement of stakeholders.

5.7.2 Example

The key information about each lesson can be captured in a simple table, where there are columns for the lesson, its impact, the recommended action and the owner. Table 5.11 shows an example for a lesson learned about the effectiveness of the project board.

Table 5.11 An example of the key information for a lesson learned

Lesson	Impact	Recommended action	Owner
The project sponsor had very little experience of project management.	There were low levels of engagement, the lack of understanding of the processes made decision-making slow and there was resistance to the structure.	Project sponsors and members of steering groups should have induction training on their role and the key terminology and concepts of project management.	Head of project management office/ centre of excellence

5.8 Role responsibilities for Delivering the Plan

The role responsibilities for this stage can be summarized as follows:

- Project sponsor

  - Providing leadership and direction in the management of obstacles

  - Actively supporting the quality management activities

  - Intervening to resolve disputes where different parts of the organization have different priorities

  - Engaging and maintaining stakeholder involvement

  - Ensuring the planned levels of controls are being applied

  - Organizing assurance reviews

- Project manager

  - Leading the re-planning activities

  - Gathering information on which to assess progress

  - Generating performance reports

  - Developing the information and documentation to support decision-making

  - Applying the controls

  - Focusing on achieving the milestone plan and the schedule

  - Engaging stakeholders in the process and maintaining communications

- **Business representative**
  - Providing operational knowledge and input to support delivery
  - Undertaking quality assessments of the products
  - Delivering the committed resources
- **Suppliers (internal or external)**
  - Providing market knowledge
  - Supplying expert advice to support specifications
  - Advising on ability to achieve within current agreements
  - Providing resources
  - Notifying quality or delivery issues to the project manager
- **Project management office/centre of excellence**
  - Advising on other projects that may be generating similar requirements
  - Advising on use of planning framework and techniques
  - Identifying cross-project dependencies and opportunities to remove or exploit, in order to gain efficiencies
  - Acting as a central repository for project information, including lessons learned
  - Reviewing project reports
  - Providing support for re-planning when required.

Appendix 1 Summary of plans

A project plan is normally made up of a number of component plans, which cover a range of specific areas that a project may need to address. This appendix is a summary of the main plans that may be required to deliver a project and the existing plans that may contribute to or affect the project plan.

In considering plans it is useful to consider 'change' and operations levels in an organization.

At the top there will be business plans with business operations activities and initiatives that will deliver the organization's medium-term finance plan. Within this plan will be 'change objectives' to be delivered by the change portfolio, and its programmes and projects. These may introduce programme or project obstacles (e.g. deadlines or periods when change cannot happen).

Here we focus on the 'change' agenda.

A programme plan's scope will include (high-level) project plans, transition plans, benefits plans and quality plans.

A project plan will include high-level stage controls and major milestones.

A stage plan will include plans for communications, resources, finance, milestones and quality control/tests. Exception plans typically replace an existing stage plan as a consequence of tolerances being exceeded.

Contingency plans are conditional risk responses that should be incorporated into stage plans as and when risks materialize into issues for which there is a pre-defined response.

There may be a specific stage plan that addresses procurement, or procurement may be part of another stage plan.

If a stage plan is at an insufficient level to deliver the products then team plans may need to be developed in more detail than the stage plan. Certain groups (e.g. construction or technology teams) may need to go into significant levels of technique detail within their own team plans.

Table A1.1 summarizes the plans that you might come across.

Table A1.1 Summary of plans

Type	Description
Benefits plan	The benefits plan is the schedule of activities that will be undertaken within the operational areas to deliver the benefits outlined in the business case. Some activities may be outside the project's control but will provide important obstacles or deadlines with which the project must work. The benefits plan may include the transition plan.
Business plan	The business operations activities and initiatives that will deliver the organization's objectives.
Communications plan	This is the schedule of communications activities that the project will deliver, which may range from simple email bulletins to full-blown publicity campaigns.
Contingency plan	A plan that exists for an event that may happen although efforts are being made to mitigate it. If the event does materialize, this plan will be activated.
Exception plan	A plan that is produced to deal with an unexpected event such as a risk or issue. It outlines how the project will deal with the challenge and the knock-on effect on the overall project plan.
Finance plan	This plan should show the schedule of expenditure, when funds will be needed, the type of funds required and what they will be spent on. It may also show income generated by the project, for example from benefits.
Milestone plan	An overarching summary of the major events of the project. The events can be illustrated by using the outcome model or a high-level product sequence diagram showing the timeline for their delivery.
Portfolio plan	A plan that sits above the programmes and projects and shows how they fit together to contribute to the organization's objectives.
Procurement plan	The procurement plan sets out the approach to procurement, resources needed, the timetable and associated events to review the options.
Programme plan	A plan that sits above the projects and illustrates the delivery of the programme, business change and realization of benefits. The project will be expected to align key outputs and outcomes with the needs of the programme.
Project plan	The project plan should provide details of resources, activities, schedules, milestones and responsibilities for achieving the objectives of the project. It should integrate the other plans within it.
Quality plan (assurance plan)	This is the schedule of activities that will assure everyone that the project is on target and delivers what is required. The quality plan should include reviews of the status of the creation of the project outputs and their fitness for purpose, configuration management, the quality of the management of the project and its compliance with organization standards, and the continuing alignment with the needs of the business that are driving it.

Table continues

Table A1.1 *continued*

Type	Description
Resource plan	This plan should identify what resources will be required to deliver what tasks and the amount of their time and effort that will be needed by the project.
Stage plan	A plan that contains details of activities and schedules that will cover the project delivery during a specific delivery stage.
Team plans	Team plans should provide a detailed schedule of activities and resources for a particular area within the project. They may be managed locally by a team manager or integrated as a subset of the project plan. A team may well be put into place to deliver a specific work package, so it could be called a work package plan if necessary.
Testing plan	The schedule of activities to test and prove the functionality and fitness for purpose of the outputs that are created as part of the project.
Transition plan	The transition plan includes the project, operational and other activities that cover the implementation of the capability delivered by the project and the support of operational delivery during this period.

Appendix 2 Project planning summary

This appendix illustrates how the examples from the publication can be pulled together into the project plan, indicating where and how the techniques are used. The summary helps you to build a 'story', which can be shared with the stakeholders as the plan develops.

A2.1 Introduction

This is where you can put a few paragraphs to explain what the business drivers are, and why the project is moving forward at this time.

A2.2 Overarching objective

With so much information available it is sometimes easy to lose sight of the project's purpose, so it is often helpful to have some simple statement of the overarching objective, sometimes called a charter, vision or mission.

A2.3 Plan definition (business requirements)

The examples used in Chapters 2 and 3 are for the development of a training programme for an organization. This is a simple example to enable people to follow the concept. In the publication we have talked about this as the stage where the plan is defined, though in the real world you may find it easier to refer to this as the business requirements stage.

A2.3.1 Objectives

This is the section where the objectives should be added. Note that you should have a variety of objectives and focus on the wider context of your planning and the overall impact you hope to have. Table 2.1 provides an example.

A2.3.2 Stakeholder analysis

This is the where you can add your stakeholder analysis (see Table 2.3), so that you have a record of who you have identified, and which areas of your project they are interested in.

A2.3.4 Categorized and prioritized business requirements

This section is a key area. It is where you can record all your research showing what the business requires, priorities etc. This could well be done by business analysts, but if they are not available, you now have the tools do a decent job. Tables 2.4, 2.6 and 2.9 show examples of how the information is gradually built up and Table 2.8 shows how the requirements can be analysed to help determine the priorities.

A2.3.5 Obstacles to be faced

If your organization has a standard approach to managing issues and risks then you should use their templates. If not, this is still a good place to log the issues and risks (obstacles) that you know you will face so it is easy for stakeholders if they are looking for them. Table 2.5 provides an example of an obstacle log.

A2.4 Plan design (outcome design)

This is the stage where you are pulling all the elements of the plan together, so it is a good place to describe the approach you are taking and the information that people will need to read. You may find it easier to call this stage 'outcome design', as it has a more general perspective for people reading it.

A2.4.1 Outcome model

An outcome model is useful so that stakeholders can get an overview of the project in one simple place; after this you will be going into more detail as you develop your plans. The model will be a useful communications tool in the future. For an example of an outcome model, see Figure 3.2.

A2.4.2 Project output breakdown structure

Now you are moving into more formal project planning, you can insert your detailed breakdown of what needs to be delivered under each heading to achieve your objectives. Figure 3.5 is an example of a product breakdown structure, while Table 3.2 shows a more detailed breakdown structure for part of Figure 3.5. An approximate sequence of events can be produced by turning the product breakdown structure on its side (see Figure 3.6).

A2.4.3 Product descriptions

Before you can commission anyone to do any work, you need to give them a description of what you require so that there is no misunderstanding. You need to do this for each product you commission. Table 3.3 provides a reminder of what content is needed in a product description and Table 3.4 is an example of this information filled in for the training course.

A2.5 Plan development (product build)

The main case study used in Chapter 4 was to implement a new IT helpline service. This is a more complex example to enable more complex techniques to be demonstrated in the text.

We have used the term 'plan development' but in reality this would be covering the development or build phase of whatever your project is planning to create. So you may find a more useful title that better fits what you do.

A2.5.1 Schedule estimate and plan for contingency

A table can be used as the start of scheduling estimates and planning for contingency. Table 4.4 demonstrates use of the three-point estimating technique to show the various cases for the helpline example.

A2.5.2 Stage plan

The stage plan summarizes the stages that the project will go through. Table 4.5 lists the stages for the helpline example, with the sorts of things that will be in scope for each stage.

A2.5.3 Milestone plan

Major outcomes identified in mapping the journey make for good milestones. Table 4.6 provides an example of milestones for the helpline project. For your own project you could add a column for dates, so the overview of the plan could be seen. You could also link the milestones back to stages.

A2.5.4 Resource plan

A detailed resource plan makes it clearly visible what people will be needed and for how long. It helps to illustrate any gaps and overlaps, and it will help departments or partners to fit in with your plan. Tables 4.7 and 4.8 provide examples for an office move.

A2.5.5 Project schedule

By adding timings into a product sequence diagram that shows dependencies and by using critical path analysis (CPA), a project schedule can be drawn up. Figures 4.6 to 4.8 and Table 4.9 illustrate this process for the helpline example.

Gantt charts (which can be produced using tables or spreadsheets as well as specialized software) are also useful to show a project schedule. For an example see Figure 4.9.

A2.5.6 Delivery controls

This is where you define how your project will be controlled to achieve its objectives. In organizations where there is a project management framework, you may just need to explain how you are going to meet the standards rather than to define them. For an example of factors to consider when designing controls, see Table 4.10.

A2.5.7 Risk management

This is the process that will be used to identify risks within the project. You may need a process model (see Figure 4.10 for an example) for each of the control areas to make sure roles and responsibilities are clear.

A2.6 Plan delivery

A2.6.1 Issue management and change control

This is the process and activities that will be used to ensure obstacles are dealt with effectively and that there is a structured way of processing changes that will affect the achievement of the project within its scope. Table 5.2 shows the steps for change control, and Table 5.3 is an example of a change request, which is an important part of documenting changes in an organized way.

A2.6.2 Stakeholder management

The key to successful stakeholder management is to set realistic expectations and then maintain engagement through regular communications that reinforce expectations at the appropriate level. You can gauge the level of stakeholder support by mapping this against objectives over time and analysing the results (see Tables 5.4 to 5.6).

A2.6.3 Time management

Time management involves comparing the reported actual schedule and progress with that established in the baseline plan and if necessary planning corrective actions to deal with problems. A variation report, such as that shown in Table 5.7, is a useful tool to see whether time estimates were accurate and within tolerance.

A2.6.4 Cost management

As with time management, the cost analysis should be based on the expected costs and tolerance that may been allocated to the project. The technique for managing costs is similar to managing time, and Table 5.8 gives an example of a cost variation report.

A2.6.5 Quality management

This is the process that will be followed to ensure that the project delivers the objectives and that there is measurable evidence of success. The quality controls will keep the project within scope and ensure that the outputs and outcomes meet the business requirements. They will also include acceptance testing of systems and tools being provided as part of the project. The quality review is the main way of assuring quality, and its techniques are outlined in Table 5.9. Table 5.10 provides an example of what to include in a quality report.

A2.6.6 Capturing lessons learned

It is unlikely that the project will go exactly as planned, but instead of regarding problems as failures they should be regarded as an opportunity to gain experience and make improvements. Lessons learned should be captured and shared with the project board and the impact of the lessons on this and other projects should be understood. Table 5.11 shows how key information for a lesson learned could be recorded.

Index

Bold page numbers indicate figures, *italic* numbers indicate tables.